D1596851

STONE AGE AFRICA

Part of a painted frieze at Cheke Rock Shelter in Tanganyika Territory
showing styles 4 (block), 5 (the thin single outline including the outline of
large animals later filled in with yellow wash), 6 (orange lines to the left),
7 (the full colour eland giraffe, and probably the human figures), 8 (the elephant in brick-red outline), and 9 (figures in conventionalized brick-red
outline—see small animal at top left).   Reduced to $\frac{1}{20}$ (approx.)

STONE AGE AFRICA

AN OUTLINE OF PREHISTORY IN AFRICA

BY

L. S. B. LEAKEY

*Each of the Chapters formed the
subject-matter of one of the ten
MUNRO LECTURES delivered in
Edinburgh, February 1936*

NEGRO UNIVERSITIES PRESS
NEW YORK

Originally published in 1936
by Oxford University Press, London

Reprinted in 1970 by
Negro Universities Press
A Division of Greenwood Press, Inc.
Westport, Connecticut

SBN 8371-2022-5

Printed in United States of America

PREFACE

WHEN I was invited to give the course of Munro lectures at Edinburgh University during the academic year 1935–6, I at first thought of devoting the whole course to a study of the Prehistory of East Africa alone, but on further consideration I decided that it would be more useful, perhaps, to try to give a general picture of the present state of our knowledge of the Stone Age over the whole African continent. In the course of preparing the lectures I learnt a very great deal myself, and I hope that in making what I learnt available to a wider public than that which attended the lectures I shall help others to understand better the relationship of the Stone Age cultures of Africa to those of Europe. Although the Munro lectures are open to the general public and had therefore to be prepared with a non-specialist audience in view, I assumed that any one who attended the course would have at least a general knowledge of, and interest in, the subject, such as may be obtained by reading any of the many semi-popular books on Prehistory. I therefore have not attempted to explain the meaning of words like Chellean, Aurignacian, &c.

In publishing the lectures in book-form I very much hope that they will prove interesting to many people, and I am encouraged in this hope by the good reception that was given to my book *Adam's Ancestors*.

For the sake of students and specialists I have given a fairly full bibliography, for they will find that my generalized account does not give them all that they want, and they will naturally wish to study much of the available evidence in detail for themselves.

The chapters which deal with regions or subjects other than those with which I am personally acquainted have been submitted to other experts for comments and criticism, and I am particularly indebted to Mr. M. C.

Burkitt, Dr. A. T. Hopwood, Professor R. Vaufrey, and Professor C. van Riet Lowe for their assistance in this respect.

To Professor van Riet Lowe I also owe much gratitude for the way in which he so kindly put certain unpublished information at my disposal so that I could make the South African story more complete and accurate.

In addition to questions of fact, I have throughout the book discussed certain theories of culture origin, of independent evolution versus diffusion, &c., and although I do not expect every one to agree with my views on these matters, I hope that they will receive careful consideration.

In conclusion I wish to thank Miss Mary Nicol for her excellent drawings of stone tools which illustrate the book, and for her help in preparation of the map and index.

L. S. B. LEAKEY.

March 1936.

ERRATA

Frontispiece: 2nd line, *for* 'block' *read* 'black'.
Table, p. 136: Under Upper Pleistocene, *for* 'Gambuan' *read* 'Gamblian'.
List of figures, 4: *for* 'Naivaska' *read* 'Naivasha'.
        22: *for* 'Burkett' *read* 'Burkitt'.
Bibliography, p. 197, 8, 10; p. 202, 2, 3, 6: *for* 'Vaufray' *read* 'Vaufrey'.

CONTENTS

LIST OF FIGURES IN THE TEXT

LIST OF PLATES

CHAPTER I
CLIMATE AND GEOGRAPHY

AT the present day the climate of Africa varies very greatly in different regions and at different seasons, and this is due to the geographical position of this immense continent.

Before we pass on to the climate and geography of the Stone Age it will be well to recall briefly present-day conditions.

The North African littoral, bounding the southern shores of the Mediterranean Sea, has a climate which is not very different from that of the southern parts of Europe to-day. Hot dry summers are common, while a wet autumn not infrequently turns to a still wetter winter, with snow-storms as an occasional feature in some places. This northern territory grades gradually southwards into the desert region of the Sahara, where the variation of temperatures is very great, especially the differences between night and day temperatures.

The Sahara desert region, broken only in the east by the fertile valley of the Nile, extends beyond the limits of the continent, right into Arabia. The intensity of desert conditions is not the same over the whole of this immense belt, but nevertheless it can all be justly described as desert belt to-day.

Southwards the desert conditions gradually give way to more vegetated country, and then this passes into the great forest and grass-land belt of the equatorial regions of the continent.

Broadly speaking, the equatorial region of Africa to-day has an abundant rainfall, but it must always be remembered that there is much evidence that desiccation is hurrying on apace to-day and that already patches of the equatorial zone are slowly becoming deserts, while over all the area the decline in rainfall presents a fairly serious problem, except perhaps in the densely forested regions of the Congo basin.

In this equatorial region the climate is by no means always what we expect it to be on the equator.

There is a great variability of altitude, and whereas in the low-lying regions the climate is truly tropical, there are in the same zone several mountains which have a permanent mantle of snow and ice, as, for example, Mounts Kilimanjaro, Kenya, and Ruenzori. Intermediate altitudes have intermediate climatic conditions. In the highlands of Kenya and Tanganyika Territory, as well as on the borders of the Congo, there are seasons of the year when the cold is intense, and the sun is seldom seen.

South of the great equatorial belt the country gradually presents a drier and drier aspect until we reach once again the great southern desert belt of the Kalahari.

For a variety of reasons which cannot be discussed here, the Kalahari desert belt is not so extensive and unbroken as the more northern African desert belt, but it is none the less a real feature of the African continent. Southwards, again, comes the more or less temperate region of South Africa, where in winter it is often very cold, and where the climate, taken as a whole, is not very different from that of the North African littoral.

The present-day physical geography cannot of course be fully discussed here, but if we are to appreciate the geography of the past, we must have a background of the present upon which to judge it.

Probably the most amazing physical feature of the continent is the Great Rift Valley, which cuts right through Africa from the Red Sea to the Zambesi River. The Red

Sea itself is a part of this great crack, which, when followed northward, can be traced right through Palestine to the sources of the Jordan River. The Great Rift Valley is marked throughout its length to-day by a chain of lakes, varying greatly in size. In the western branch of the Rift (for in Central Africa it divides into two main branches) the lakes are for the most part far greater than those in the eastern branch.

Lying between the two Rift Valley branches on the equator is Africa's greatest lake, Victoria Nyanza, which is approximately equal in extent to the country òf Ireland.

Running right down the eastern side of the continent from Abyssinia almost to the Cape of Good Hope is a highland belt, which follows practically the same line as that of the Great Rift Valley. This 'backbone' of Africa, as it is often called, is by no means unconnected with the Great Rift Valley, and the fact that the two lines are to all intents and purposes the same is probably more than mere coincidence.

Along the line of this 'backbone' of Africa there are many giant extinct volcanoes, which in some cases form great mountain ranges and in others stand as isolated sentinels.

But if extinct volcanoes are so common, active ones are rare in Africa at the present day, although this quiescence may be only temporary.

Among many great African rivers three must be especially mentioned in connexion with the present-day geography of Africa, because, as we shall see presently, they loom large in the picture of the geography of Africa in Stone Age times.

The Nile to-day has two main sources of its water-supply. The White Nile rises in that great lake, Victoria Nyanza, and also draws water from Lake Albert and other lesser lakes. The other branch of the Nile, known as the Blue Nile, rises in the highlands of Abyssinia in the region of Lake Tsana.

The Zambesi River is important in present-day African geography because, among other reasons, it gives us Africa's most spectacular Falls, the Victoria Falls.

The Vaal River is the other great river of importance to our study, but it must not be thought that these are the only really great rivers of Africa. Mighty river systems, like those of the Congo and the Niger, are very important features of present-day African geography, but at present, at any rate, they do not concern us very much, as we are only interested in the present as a background for our study of the past, and the past history of these and many other rivers of Africa is still shrouded in mystery.

Let us now turn from the present to the past and see something of what the climate and physical geography of Africa was like during the time that Stone Age man held sway over the continent.

The most important aspects of the changes that have taken place are linked with the following subjects: the relative changes of land- and sea-level all round the shores of the African continent; the great volcanic activity which has occurred during the period, and which has been responsible for great changes on the face of Africa; the very great earth movements to which the continent has been subjected and which have given rise not only to the Great Rift Valley in the form in which we know it to-day, but also to all sorts of secondary changes; the very marked changes of climate which can be linked to some extent with similar world-wide changes, and which in Africa gave rise to alternate very wet and very arid periods; these climatic changes have been responsible for vast geographical changes.

PLATE 1

A view of the gorge below the Victoria Falls on the Zambesi river.
This gorge has been cut since the Middle Pleistocene period

All of these aspects of our problem must be briefly discussed and some of the evidence for them given, but I shall not attempt to go into great detail, for to do so would involve the writing of a whole book instead of one short chapter in a small book.

Even where the African continent is concerned the discovery that there have been very great changes in relative land- and sea-level in human times is not a new one. Years ago students of the history of the Mediterranean Sea noticed that all along the northern shores of that sea there were a series of old high-level beaches, whose origin was by no means remote when judged by geological standards. These changes have been studied by many scientists in great detail, and at first the theory was advanced that during this period of oscillation of land- and sea-level there were times when land-bridges connected Europe and Africa. More recently, various workers, especially Dr. R. Vaufrey of Paris, have put forward the view that although the evidences of relative changes of sea-level are quite beyond dispute, there is no evidence at all that these hypothetical land-bridges existed during the latter part of the Pleistocene period.[1]

On the other hand, more and more workers have shown that the high-level beaches which fringe the northern coast of the Mediterranean have their counterpart along the coast of North Africa, and there is abundant evidence that, during some at least of the changes, man was present in North Africa, as we shall see in a later chapter.

[1] Professor Vaufrey is inclined to go farther and to suggest that there were no Mediterranean land-bridges at any time during the Pleistocene, but evidence which will appear elsewhere in the book seems to indicate clearly that there were land-bridges in the earlier part of the Pleistocene, but not later.

Nor were these changes of sea-level restricted to the inland waters of the Mediterranean.

Just as these changes are known to have affected the whole of the western shores of Europe, so, too, traces of such changes have been recorded at many points round the African continent. This means that without a doubt during the period of the Stone Age there were immense changes going on over the whole area. At Mombasa, on the east coast of Africa, there is ample evidence that at times the sea-level stood much higher than it does to-day, and there are to be found marine deposits containing Stone Age man's tools at levels considerably above the present-day high-water mark.

In South Africa—for example, at Mossel-Bay—there are old marine beaches containing stone tools, and similar evidence is now coming to light at many places round the African continent.

But whereas it is certain that these movements of the old shore-lines have occurred, it is by no means certain to what causes these changes are to be attributed. There are some scientists who believe that the locking-up of vast amounts of water in the form of ice sheets in the northern and southern hemispheres during the glacial periods can be made to account for the progressive lowering of the sea-level, but if this is so then the sea-level should now be rising again in relation to the land-level, for at present we are in one of the stages of an interglacial period, and the ice sheets of the north and south are still retreating. It is, of course, just possible—though uncertain —that when an interglacial period is at its maximum all the ice sheets of the Arctic and Antarctic regions melt away.

But, supposing this to be the case, is it at all certain that there is enough water locked up in these regions as ice caps to bring the levels of seas and oceans all over the world up to heights recorded in prehistoric times? The answer is that we do not know, but it is doubtful.

Another explanation that is often put forward to explain the high-level beaches of Europe is that the weight of the ice sheets which advanced over the continent depressed the level of the earth's surface and in this way allowed the seas to cut beaches high above the present sea-level. This theory has not a few supporters as far as Europe is concerned, but it falls to the ground when we try to apply it to Africa, for the African continent never had extensive ice sheets in human times. Moreover, the fact that this theory is inapplicable for Africa deprives it of much of its value as applied to Europe, for, as I have already said, there is evidence to show that as far as the Mediterranean basin is concerned the phenomenon applied to both Africa and south Europe. If the high-level beaches of south Europe were due to a pressing-down of that continent by the weight of ice sheets, then on the southern shores of the Mediterranean there should be no contemporary raised beaches. Therefore we have probably got to look elsewhere for an explanation of the relative changes of land- and sea-level which were not restricted to one area, but were practically universal.

As we shall see presently, there is abundant evidence for great convulsive earth-movements during the Pleistocene period, and I personally believe that we shall one day be able to show that these great earth-movements can be directly linked up with the changes of land- and sea-level both in Africa and Europe, but it must be clearly understood that there is at present no positive proof for such a belief. I shall, however, endeavour in the last chapter of this book to show that where absolute proof is wanting much suggestive evidence is available.

Although to-day there are very few active volcanoes in Africa, the number of volcanoes of very recent origin is enormous, and to-day we have a great deal of evidence to show that the period of the Stone Age in Africa coincided with a period of very great volcanic activity. This activity was very largely connected with the violent earth-movements which shook Africa during the same period, some of the volcanic eruptions preceding these movements and making the beginning of new disturbances, and others following upon the faulting movements.

As a result of these volcanic eruptions the physical geography of Africa was very considerably changed. Mountains and mountain ranges were built up where formerly there were none. Lava sheets extruded from fissures in the earth's surface and spread over the country-side, while great mantles of volcanic ash and dust were spread over existing land-surfaces in such a way as materially to alter their configuration.

It is in East Africa that these phenomena have been most studied, and yet even there we know extraordinarily little of the details, and a very big specialized field of work is awaiting some keen research worker who is interested in this particular branch of study.

The proof of the fact that much of the volcanicity occurred long after Stone Age man was well established in Africa is to be found in the fact that in many cases lava sheets, and great masses of volcanic ash and pumice, are found overlying deposits which contain Stone Age tools in abundance.

The great eruptions of this time were closely linked up with the earth-movements which gave rise to the Great Rift Valley in its present form.

Until comparatively recently it was held that the formation of the Great Rift Valley long antedated the period of

PLATE II

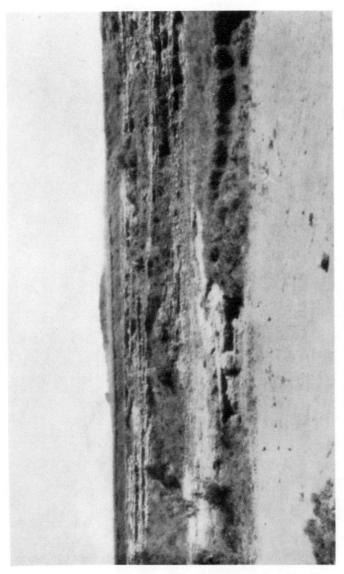

A view of the stratified lake beds at the top of the Kinangop Plateau. These are cut through by the major faulting of the Great Rift Valley (see also Figs. 4, 5, and 6 in connexion with this photograph)

human occupation of Africa, but now we know that many of the greatest movements which gave rise to it occurred in human times. There is clear evidence now of three distinct periods of faulting during the Pleistocene period. These are best known from the studies of Mr. E. J. Wayland in Uganda, but there is much similar evidence from Kenya Colony, Tanganyika Territory, and Nyasaland.

Even in North Africa, Professor Vaufrey has recently shown that there were earth-movements of considerable severity during the Pleistocene. It must not be supposed that there was no trace of a Great Rift Valley before the human period. On the contrary, there is not a little evidence to show that along certain sections of the Great Rift Valley faulting goes back to a very remote period, but what would now seem to be certain is that the most severe faulting took place at three distinct points in the Pleistocene period and that, moreover, of these three the most severe was the last, which occurred a very long time after man had been living and evolving in the district (see Chapter III).

Wherever the matter has been investigated in recent times, evidence has been found that some of the fault scarps of the Great Rift Valley *cut through* deposits which contain Stone Age man's tools, thus proving beyond question the recent age of some, at least, of the faulting. The most remarkable instances of this are to be found in Kenya, Uganda, and Tanganyika Territory. In Kenya the 2,000-foot cliffs of the Great Rift Valley near Naivasha are found to cut right through old lake and marsh deposits which yield abundant stone implements. At the Oldoway Gorge in Tanganyika Territory a remarkable series of old lake deposits about 300 feet in thickness are, in many places, cut through by faults. These deposits are very rich in relics of human occupation.

In Uganda Mr. E. J. Wayland has found similar evidence, and in Nyasaland Dr. Dixie has also reported the finding of great Pleistocene faults.

Associated with the Great Rift Valley faulting there is a great deal of evidence of an uplifting of extensive areas of the earth's crust in Africa, during Stone Age times. These 'uplift' movements have had many results, and have considerably changed the geography of the whole country affected. In Uganda Mr. E. J. Wayland has proved that the river systems were reversed on several occasions in human times, and the same is true of other countries in Africa. In Kenya the uplifting has resulted in the raising of the altitude of many areas, and as more research is carried out we shall, I feel certain, find that similar movements can be traced all over Africa.

We must turn next to the changes of climate which have occurred in human times in Africa.

The study of this question is still in its infancy, but we already know a great deal. There is indisputable evidence from very many parts of the continent which shows that there have been a succession of alternating wet and dry periods, which are now termed pluvial and interpluvial periods. Once again it is in East Africa (Kenya, Uganda, and Tanganyika Territory) that most of the work on this subject has been carried out, but already there is a vast amount of contributory evidence from other parts of Africa, more especially Egypt and the Nile Valley, North Africa, and South Africa.[1]

In East Africa the evidence which has been accumulating since 1919 now shows fairly certainly that there were three main pluvial periods followed by two less important wet phases. The first of these pluvial periods has not

[1] A paper summarizing the climatic changes of Africa appeared in *Man* for February 1936 after this book was already written.

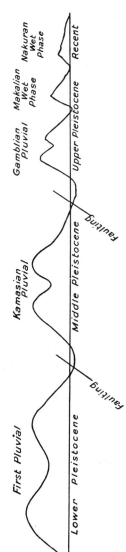

FIG. 1. Graph to indicate the climatic changes in East Africa according to the author.

yet been named, but the second is known as the Kamasian Pluvial, the third as the Gamblian Pluvial, while the later minor wet phases are known as Makalian and Nakuran respectively.

In South Africa the study of the various great rivers such as the Vaal River and the Zambesi shows quite clearly that there are a number of river terraces at various heights above the present-day level of the river, which seem to indicate periods of greater humidity. These terraces contain in their gravels many Stone Age implements. In North Africa the study of the fauna of the earlier part of the Stone Age, as well as of river terraces, shows, too, that there were periods when the climate was much wetter, and the same is true of Egypt and the Nile Valley, of parts of West Africa and of Nyasaland, &c.

A number of attempts have been made to establish exact correlations between the pluvial and interpluvial periods of Africa on the one hand, and the glacial and interglacial periods of Europe on the other. That there is some correlation no one can doubt, but the exact nature of that correlation is still not certain. At all events, it is reasonable to believe that both the glacial and the pluvial periods were the result of some great world change of climate.

If we leave Europe out of account, we still know (largely as a result of the excellent work done by Dr. Erik Nilsson) that during the pluvial periods in Africa the mean temperature level was lower, so that ice caps were able to be formed on many mountains, at much lower levels than is possible with the climate as it is at present.

On such of Africa's mountains as still have an ice cap—as, for example, Mounts Kenya, Kilimanjaro, and the various peaks of the Ruenzori group—there is now plenty of evidence that the snow and ice line formerly extended down to about the 10,000-foot level, whereas to-day it is normally restricted to altitudes above 14,000 feet.

Similarly, on many mountain masses with an altitude of more than 10,000 and less than 14,000 feet, and which to-day have no ice caps, Dr. Nilsson and others have found evidence of former glaciers and snow caps. Moreover, there is evidence to show that these local glaciations were contemporary with the pluvial periods.

As may well be imagined, the effect of pluvial periods, with the implied increase of rainfall, was to alter the geography of the country not a little, and the fact that the pluvial periods were accompanied by a lowering of the mean temperature level assisted, as this meant that evaporation was reduced.

Among the many geographical changes resulting from the pluvial periods we can only here mention a few. The levels of a great many lakes were raised considerably, and the traces of this can be found all over Africa in the form of old beach lines high up above present-day lake level in many lake basins, and also in the presence of vast accumulations of old lake deposits, beds of gravels, sands, silts, and clays laid down in high-level lakes in present-day lake basins as well as in many parts of the continent where under the climatic conditions of to-day no lakes exist at all.

Lake Rudolph, which lies in the desert region in the north of Kenya Colony, was in pluvial times a much bigger lake and its waters apparently overflowed northwards and linked up with the Nile. In fact, Lake Rudolph, which is to-day completely isolated, was formerly probably one of the chief sources of the Nile.

Down at Oldoway at the south-east corner of the Serengeti Plains, there are, as we have seen above, extensive lake deposits in an area which is to-day practically a desert. Scientists who have visited Lake Chad in north-west Africa say that it is but a shrunken pool, compared with its former extent. In Rhodesia a study of the famous Victoria Falls of the Zambesi River shows that that river has cut back a deep gorge of about ten miles in length in human times. This can most easily be explained if we think of a river with a very much greater and more power-ful flow of water than it has even to-day, although prob-ably other factors have also played their part in this case.

Nor are the changes of climate only evidenced by a study of geological phenomena. It is a most interesting fact that the study of living faunas and their distribution over Africa entirely bears out the other evidence of pluvial periods. A few examples must suffice to show the nature of this type of evidence.

When the Zoological Expedition under Dr. E. B. Worthington studied the fauna of Lake Rudolph they found that it was essentially a Nile fauna, although so completely cut off from the Nile to-day. And, as this fauna has not altered greatly, the evidence shows that the linkage with the Nile must have been recent, for if such a fauna had been isolated for a long period it would have become modified.

Ornithologists studying the distribution of various species of birds have found that their present range can only be explained by suggesting that not so very long ago the forest areas were far more extensive and linked up many forest regions which are now virtually islands. This is entirely in keeping with our belief in pluvial periods, for pluvial periods must have meant more forest regions, and, indeed, the study of fossil faunas, as we shall see in the next chapter, reveals many forest forms in areas where to-day no forests exist.

Similarly, mammalian specialists can only explain the

distribution of animals such as the potto and the bongo by arguing that the forest areas were, comparatively recently, much more extensive than they are to-day.

Even during the minor wet phases which succeeded the pluvial periods the climate of Africa was sufficiently different from to-day to have a marked effect not only upon physical geography but also upon fauna and the movement of peoples. As we shall see in later chapters, as recently as about 3,000 years ago it was possible for late Stone Age people who had acquired a knowledge of agriculture to live in agricultural communities in regions where to-day such activities are out of the question owing to the lack of water. Similarly the study of the fauna of regions such as North Africa at the close of the Stone Age shows that various animals could flourish in regions where to-day the climate is too dry for them. Many African lakes which to-day, owing to evaporation, have a very high soda content and are undrinkable, are found to have had human occupation sites on their shores during the closing stages of the Pleistocene, showing that the waters had still not acquired too great an alkalinity.

We may summarize the climatic and geographical changes which have taken place in Africa during the Stone Age as follows.

The relative levels of land and sea have altered on a number of occasions, and these changes of level seem to be linked with similar changes round the coast of Europe, so that there is good reason to believe that they were an expression of some world-wide changes, the causes of which are still not fully understood.

The climate of Africa underwent a series of oscillations from very wet to dry and sometimes even arid conditions. These climatic changes, which are known as pluvial and interpluvial periods, are comparable to the European changes of climate known as glacial and interglacial periods. Although no direct correlation is as yet possible on more than a hypothetical basis, there is every reason to believe that both the European and African climatic pulsations are merely expressions of a world-wide series of events. In other words, there is now every reason for believing that during the period of the Stone Age the climate of the world was affected by something (possibly major changes of solar radiation) which resulted in affecting the climates of all regions.

The geography of Africa was very materially altered not only as a result of the climatic changes, but also by very great earth movements which were accompanied by great volcanic activity. There were three main periods of faulting, the last of which was the most intense. In addition to an accompaniment of volcanic activity the faulting is intimately linked with considerable uplift movements and also with the formation of depressions (as distinct from faults) such as that which contains Lake Victoria. The climatic changes had a very great effect upon the flora and fauna of the continent, as is shown by a study of the present-day zoology and botany.

The study of the climate and geography of Africa is still in its infancy, and a very great deal of detailed work awaits those qualified and willing to undertake it. It is a study of fundamental importance, as it provides the only possible background against which a proper investigation and reconstruction of the Stone Age can be carried out.

CHAPTER II

THE FAUNA OF THE STONE AGE

GEOLOGISTS have divided geological time into a number of divisions, but we are concerned only with the last two of these in this book: the Pleistocene and the Holocene (or Recent).

The various periods are each characterized by fossil remains of different organisms, and, in fact, it may be said that, in general, a study of the fauna of any given geological deposit is the surest way of determining its age.[1] It is for this reason that fossil animal remains are of so great an importance to those who investigate the story of prehistoric man, and this chapter will be devoted to a discussion of the fauna of Africa during the Stone Age, and of its significance.

Unfortunately, there is still no absolute agreement among geologists and palaeontologists as to the exact definition of the Pleistocene and the Recent periods. The definition which I accept personally, and one which seems to be gradually gaining ground, states that the dawn of the Pleistocene period is marked by the appearance for the first time of true elephants, true horses, and true oxen. I have discussed and supported this definition in several publications, so that I need not enlarge upon it now, save to point out once more that it is the only definition of the Pleistocene which has a more or less world-wide application, with the important exceptions of the continent of Australia, the island of Madagascar, and other similarly isolated lands.

Some geologists hold that we are still in the Pleistocene

---

[1] Each geographical region must, however, be studied independently, as otherwise serious mistakes may arise.

C

period and they therefore leave the period called Holocene or Recent out of account, but the more generally accepted view seems to be that the Pleistocene ends and the Holocene begins at about the time when domesticated cattle and sheep first appeared.[1]

As there is still a good deal of confusion in connexion with the use of faunas for dating purposes, and as I must plead guilty to having misused and misunderstood the value of faunas in the past, I wish to make certain comments here which have a very special bearing upon Africa. Before the age of any deposit can be assessed upon the basis of the fauna contained in it, it is necessary to have as large and representative a collection as possible from that deposit, and the age must then be judged not by reference to the oldest and most archaic forms in the assemblage, but rather by the newest forms.

Let me illustrate this by examples. In various parts of Africa to-day rivers and lakes are laying down deposits of silts and gravels which contain the bones of such animals as giraffes, rhinoceroses, and elephants, archaic animals which have succeeded in persisting up to the present day. Those rivers and lakes are also burying in the same deposits the bones of sheep and cattle, and it is obviously these which in the future will have to be used in assessing the age of the deposits.

Let us look at the question another way. In Europe animals such as elephants, hyaenas, hippopotami, lions, and rhinoceroses have long since become extinct, and as a detailed study of the different extinct forms has been carried out it is possible to use the fossil remains of some

[1] The earliest domestic cattle go back to about 5000 B.C. or even earlier, but in some parts of the world they do not appear until a few thousands of years later. In terms of geological time, however, domestic cattle may be regarded as appearing simultaneously everywhere.

of these animals for dating purposes *in Europe*. But in Africa species of all of these animals are still living, and in a few cases the living African forms are not even easily distinguishable from the extinct European ones. In other words, many of the living African wild animals are what in Europe would be regarded as typically Pleistocene species. But this does not mean that time has lagged behind in Africa and that Africa is still Pleistocene while Europe is Holocene. It means rather that owing to special conditions, such as a more equable climate, rather more Pleistocene species of animals have survived in Africa than in Europe, where Pleistocene species which have survived are far less numerous, but include foxes, bears, wolves, and, of course, man.

Before we discuss the animals that lived in various parts of Africa during the Stone Age we must review the present-day fauna of Africa, for only so can we appreciate the significance of the past faunas.

Speaking very broadly, the fauna of the African continent to-day falls into three major groups, as follows: (1) the fauna of Africa north of the Sahara desert; (2) the fauna of the Congo and West Africa; and (3) the fauna of East, Central, and South Africa.

To a certain extent the faunas of all three areas do, of course, overlap, but each area has certain species which are typical of it and which do not occur in the other areas.

Let us take the North African area first of all. Species which occur in the North African area and which do not occur in the other African areas include the following: *Macacus inuus*, the Barbary ape, well known as being the only living species of monkey wild in Europe—where, however, it is restricted to the Rock of Gibraltar. *Sus scrofa*, the wild boar. *Cervus elaphus barbarus*, the North African deer. This is an animal closely related to the

Scottish red deer, and it is the only deer now living wild in Africa which appears to have been there for any length of time. The fallow deer, *Cervus dama*, is also found wild in North Africa to-day, but it is generally believed to have been imported by the Romans.

Equus asinus Africanus, the wild ass, is a native of North Africa, and so far as I know is not found wild in any other part of Africa except Somaliland. True rabbits do not occur wild in the other two areas of Africa, but in North Africa they occur, and are, indeed, supposed to have been reintroduced to Europe (where they had once existed) from North Africa.

In addition to these species which are still living wild in North Africa and which do not occur in the other two regions, mention must be made of two other species which, although they do *not* now occur wild in North Africa, have occurred there so recently that they can be included in the present day as distinct from the Pleistocene fauna. These two species are the bear and the true wild sheep, both of which were still present as wild animals at the very end of the Stone Age in Neolithic times, and even possibly later.

In addition to all these animals, which belong especially to the North African region, there is a number of species living in the same area which occur also in the others. The chief among these are the carnivores such as the lion, leopard, cheetah, serval cat, caracal, striped hyaena, and a number of small animals such as wild cats, jackals, &c. The antelopes and gazelles are mostly of species allied to those in one or both of the other regions, but are distinct and in some ways might be regarded as being special to this region.

Turning next to the region which includes the Congo and West Africa, we find that this again has certain animals which occur in it but not in either of the other two areas to-day. Chief among these are the great anthropoid apes—the gorillas and chimpanzees, both of which occur, however, in the *western* part of Uganda, which really belongs to our region No. (2) and not to the third region. Besides the anthropoid apes, the animals restricted to the second region to-day (but not necessarily occurring all over it), are the okapi, the pygmy hippopotamus, and a few smaller forest animals.

Many of the carnivora and antelopes, as well as buffaloes, monkeys, and the only species of elephant which still lives in Africa, are common to both the second and third regions.

The true wild boar, *Sus scrofa*, does not occur at all, but instead the pigs of the second region are the giant forest hogs, wart-hogs, and bush pigs, all of which also are found in the third region, as are rhinoceroses.

Typical of the third region are giraffes, zebras, wildebeest, kudu, together with a whole host of animals closely related to those found in one or both of the other areas.

When we examine each of the three faunas critically, we find that the northern region has a good many animals which are not really essentially African, for example, the deer, bear, wild sheep, and wild boar, all of which are of European or Asiatic affinities.

The second region is especially the stronghold of purely forest species, a few of which, however, also extend into forested patches in the third region, as, for example, the giant forest hog, the pottos, the bongo, and the more typically forest monkeys.

The animals of the third region are to-day almost all of them genuinely African species, although a few, such as the lions, leopards, and striped hyaenas, occur in Asia as well as Africa. (All of them, incidentally, are animals which occur in all three African regions.)

The object of this discussion of the distribution of the species living in Africa to-day may not seem at first to have any great bearing upon the real subject of this chapter, which is the fauna of the Stone Age times in Africa, but now, as we turn to the past, we shall begin to see why it was necessary to do so. At present we know practically nothing at all about the extinct fauna of our second region, so that will have to be left out of account, and we must examine in turn the first and third regions.

Records of fossil remains of extinct animals belonging to the Pleistocene period in North Africa go back as far as 1845, and from then onwards there have been a large number of notes published referring to the extinct fauna of North Africa. The best summary is that made by Dr. A. S. Romer and published in 1928 under the title of *Pleistocene Mammals of Algeria*,[1] while other summaries occur in numerous French publications.

In his paper Dr. Romer not only summarizes what is known of the North African Pleistocene animals, but he also gives a very full and valuable bibliography. More recently, in Mémoire No. 13 of the Archives of the Institute of Human Palaeontology of Paris (1934), Professor Arambourg has also reviewed the same material, and it is primarily from these two sources that I have obtained the facts which follow.

The oldest deposits which are attributed to the Pleistocene have not as yet yielded any stone implements, but this may in large part be due to the fact that the earliest human culture recognized in North Africa is the Chellean, which—as we know from evidence both in Europe and in East Africa—is far from being the oldest of human Stone

[1] Bulletin of the Belloit College, vol. xxvi, no. 5, 1928.

Age cultures. It seems more than likely that future investigation at the older Pleistocene sites in North Africa will yield cultures of a pre-Chellean type. In these oldest Pleistocene deposits the fauna list includes two species of primitive elephants, and a *Mastodon*, a species of *Hipparion*, or three-toed horse, a short-necked giraffid, a zebra, and a big horse, a pygmy hippopotamus as well as a large species, an eland and an oryx, as well as several other antelopes and gazelles, and the living African species of white rhinoceros. Unfortunately none of the sites of this early period has yielded a very rich fauna, so that the list is incomplete and obviously does not represent anything like the full number of species which were present at that time. Nevertheless, it is sufficiently full to be of very real interest. It shows us that in North Africa both the *Mastodon* and the three-toed horse persisted on into the Pleistocene period which, as we shall see presently, was also the case in East Africa, and it shows us, too, that not a few of the species which are still flourishing in Africa to-day were already fully evolved in the Lower Pleistocene period. This fact has a very important bearing upon the study of prehistory, and upon the whole question of dating by extinct animals.

Turning next to the fauna which is found in North Africa in association with the stone tools belonging to the great Chelleo-Acheulean hand-axe culture, we find that a number of species which occurred in the earlier period have disappeared altogether. The most important of these are the *Mastodon*, the *Hipparion*, the primitive elephants (which are replaced by a more evolved form), the short-necked giraffe, and the pygmy hippopotamus. As against this we have the appearance, apparently for the first time, of the true giraffe, the wildebeest, the more evolved elephant, a true wild sheep, a deer, and a bear. Unfortunately, the

fossiliferous sites of this period also are comparatively
few, so that once again we cannot regard the fauna list as
at all complete, and some of the species at present said not
to have survived into this period may possibly be found
when more is known.

The most important fact which emerges from a study
of the fauna which is contemporary with the hand-axe
culture in North Africa is that several of the forms which
appear for the first time are of European or Asiatic origin,
as, for example, the deer, wild sheep, and bear. This fact
has in the past been taken to indicate the presence of a
land-bridge across the Mediterranean at this period, and
when it is combined with the evidence of the distribution
of the great Chelleo-Acheulean culture it certainly seems
to support the view that there was at least one land-bridge
at this time, although the faunal evidence alone could
equally well be explained by postulating migrations via
Palestine and the North African littoral. The cultural
evidence will be given in another chapter.

Following the period in which the hand-axe cultures
dominate the scene in North Africa, we come to a period
during which a flake culture, allied to that called Mousterian in Europe, is the most common.

The fauna list of this period is far larger and more
comprehensive than the preceding ones, and the number
of sites from which fauna of this period has been recorded
in North Africa is correspondingly greater.

Amongst the species which appear on the scene for the
first time in this area are a Euro-Asiatic rhinoceros
(*R. mercki*), the striped hyaena, which is probably of
Asiatic origin, the fox, the pygmy elephant of the Mediterranean, the wart-hog, and another deer (*Cervus algericus*).
With the exception of the wart-hog all of these new forms
seem to have come in along the northern littoral from

Europe or Asia, and not from south of the Sahara. This seems to be a significant fact and suggests rather that there was some sort of barrier preventing the northward movement of the main African fauna of this period. (Even the wart-hog may have come from Palestine.)

It is noticeable that by this time the elephant which occurred in·deposits belonging to the preceding period, *Elephas atlanticus*, has become very rare, there being in fact only one record of it, and that specimen may well be a derived fossil. On the other hand, the true African elephant has not yet appeared. It is also noticeable that many species which are still present in other regions of Africa to-day were then living in North Africa in contact with forms of European origin.

The next period marks the final stage of the Pleistocene. In many respects the fauna is the same as that of the preceding period, but it is noticeable that many species which like a well-watered country have disappeared. Among these we may note, in particular, the disappearance of the buffalo, hippopotamus, and water-buck. To quote from Dr. Romer: 'It would appear that following the Mousterian a period of aridity set in with the loss from the local fauna of a considerable African element.' There is evidence that some sort of elephant was present at this time, but no exact identification has been made. It is, however, considered probable that it was the same as the modern African elephant. The arid period referred to above gradually gave way again to a moister climate, and in the beginning of what is known as the Holocene (or Recent) period, when the last of the truly Stone Age culture stages, the Neolithic, was present, the fauna was again reinforced from farther south by such animals as the hippopotamus, giraffe, water-buck, eland, zebra, and hyaena. This fresh movement from the south not only postulates wetter conditions in North Africa itself, but also indicates that the climate of the Sahara must have been much wetter in order that this faunal migration could take place, and direct evidence in support of this is now available from several sites (see Chapter VI).

Since the time of the Neolithic culture stage the climate of North Africa has again been growing progressively drier, and with this renewed desiccation, which is apparently still going on, many of the animals just mentioned have again died out.

In the last chapter we discussed briefly the changes of climate and geography in Africa during the Stone Age, and we saw that there was very little direct evidence—evidence of the kind which has been obtained in East Africa, for example—of great changes of climate in North Africa. The evidence of the fauna, however, makes up for this to some extent, and from the faunal succession we find that the period before the evolution of the Chellean hand-axe culture, as well as the period in which the great Chelleo-Acheulean culture flourished, were both times when a fauna characteristic of a wet climate were present. The fact that in an interval between these two periods a number of species died out altogether rather suggests that there was a drier climatic break, but the evidence is not sufficient to prove this.

The next period is marked by the arrival of many European species, while the number of more typically African forms is also increased. This may in part be due to the fact that the fauna of this period is better known, but cannot be wholly explained in that way. There is evidence that the climate was getting drier and many of the more typically African animals which came up to the North African littoral at this time probably moved northward from the Sahara region which was gradually changing from a wet to a desert area. The desiccation continued, and in time affected the whole North African littoral, killing off all those species which can only flourish in wet lands, while the gazelles and other animals capable of withstanding much drier conditions survived. Then, as we have just seen, wet conditions followed once again which very gradually have given way to the present-day climate.

This story, although less complete and exact than that which has been worked out for Central East Africa, nevertheless fits in with it remarkably well and is supported by the geological evidence of the climatic changes which have been obtained in the eastern part of North Africa by Miss Caton Thompson, Miss Gardiner, Dr. Sandford, and others.

Since little or nothing is known yet of the Pleistocene faunas of our second region, we must now turn to our third.

As far as this is concerned, by far the best documented area is East Central Africa, where Kenya Colony, Uganda Protectorate, and Tanganyika Territory have yielded a fairly complete story, which, however, has not yet been fully published.

As one of those who has been partly responsible for the collection of this East African material I can, however, give an outline of what we know here, and in doing so must express my indebtedness for much help from my friends, Professor Reck and Dr. A. T. Hopwood.

During the earliest part of the Pleistocene in East Africa, when the culture of Stone Age man is represented only by the crudest of tools of pebble type, the fauna included the following animals: very primitive true elephants; *Mastodons*, of probably two distinct species; a very large *Deinotherium*, a large equid, as well as *Hipparion*, the three-toed horse, a small species of hippopotamus, as well as one or more large species, the ordinary black rhinoceros, which is, however, rare, and the white rhinoceros which is common, a short-necked and antlered giraffid in addition to true giraffes, a number of different members of the pig family, and, in addition, a variety of antelopes and bovines as yet undetermined. In a great many ways this fauna compares fairly closely with that recorded for North Africa at the same time. The presence of *Mastodon* and *Hipparion* in association with true but primitive elephants is the same. The presence of a short-necked giraffe and of a small species of hippopotamus, too, agrees very well, but, on the other hand, the Deinotherium is not yet known to have been present in the north.

Towards the close of the period during which the primitive pebble culture flourished and before the dawn of the great Chelleo-Acheulean hand-axe culture, we have considerably more evidence of what the fauna was like, for the lowest part of the now famous Oldoway fossil beds of Tanganyika Territory belongs to this time. Here we find that the more primitive elephants have given way to the type of elephant known as *Elephas antiquus*, but at the same time the Deinotherium persists. There is no direct evidence that *Mastodons* were there, although there is some reason to believe that they too had persisted. In addition to the other animals already listed above, we can add—from what we know at Oldoway—that the fauna included a large *Chalicotherium*, a large-antlered short-necked giraffe, and a true zebra.

The time during which the hand-axe culture was evolving is now represented by a very extensive fauna in our collections, and the list is remarkable in two ways. First of all, we find that animals such as the three-toed horse, *Hipparion*, persisted right on up to the time of the

PLATE III

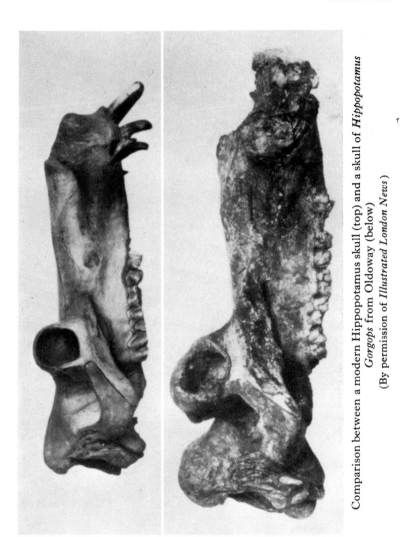

Comparison between a modern Hippopotamus skull (top) and a skull of *Hippopotamus Gorgops* from Oldoway (below)

(By permission of *Illustrated London News*)

final stages of the Acheulean, and secondly we find that a large number of the species represented have very marked Asiatic affinities. This can easily be explained by the assumption that geographical and climatic conditions at this time were such that there was probably no barrier between East Africa and Arabia eastwards to India, so that animals could range freely over this whole area, and in the preceding chapter some of the evidence supporting this view has already been given.

Although it is not yet possible to give a complete list of the fauna of the Middle Pleistocene period in East Africa, the following notes will perhaps be useful. So far the remains of fifty-one mammals have been recognized, including twenty-five extinct species and fifteen extinct genera.

The survival of such animals as *Hipparion*, the three-toed horse, *Chalicotherium*, a curious and very unusual ungulate which in Europe died out long before the Pleistocene, and *Deinotherium*, an aberrant cousin of the elephants, shows us clearly that as to-day, so in the past, many animals were present which belonged really to an earlier period. It is just for this reason that caution—which I stressed at the beginning of the chapter—is so necessary in determining the age of fossil beds in Africa from their contained fossils. If we only possessed an incomplete series of fossils from Oldoway, for example, there would be a strong risk of dating it far too early because of the presence of such animals as those just mentioned, and it is by the more evolved forms such as *Elephas antiquus* that the date has to be gauged. But here another word of warning is necessary. It might at first be argued that because certain deposits (such as those at Oldoway, for example) contain the remains of animal species which are still living to-day, therefore the deposits were of recent and not of Pleistocene date at all. Such a line of argument would be as erroneous as the opposite one of arguing that because Deinotherium is present the age must be Pliocene. It can be proved on purely *geological* grounds that animals like giraffe, zebra, wildebeest, and eland were in existence at an early date in the Pleistocene, so that their presence as fossils in any deposit does not at all necessarily mean that that deposit is modern. All that can be said is that in so far as they are Pleistocene species and not Pliocene ones, their presence shows that the deposits in which they occur *are not older* than the Pleistocene, while the actual age must be judged by studying the assemblage as a whole.

Among the more interesting of the animals with Asiatic affinities which were living in East Africa during the time that the hand-axe culture flourished, we may mention the gigantic sheep-like animal which has been named *Pelorovis*. The remains of this animal were first found in 1913 by Professor Reck, and since then my expeditions have recovered more material representing the animal. The wild sheep that was living in North Africa at the same time was more related to the South European wild sheep than to the Asiatic ones, while *Pelorovis* belongs more nearly to the group which includes the North Indian species.

The large, short-necked, antlered giraffid from East Africa, too, is closely related to Sivatherium from India, while the elephant which is typical of the period is, as we have seen, *Elephas antiquus*, which is usually regarded as a European and Asiatic form and is quite distinct from the living African species. It is, incidentally, a rather remarkable fact that so far no forms truly ancestral to the African elephant have been found anywhere; neither in the fossil beds of the African continent, nor elsewhere.

We have already seen in the first chapter that the pluvial

PLATE IV

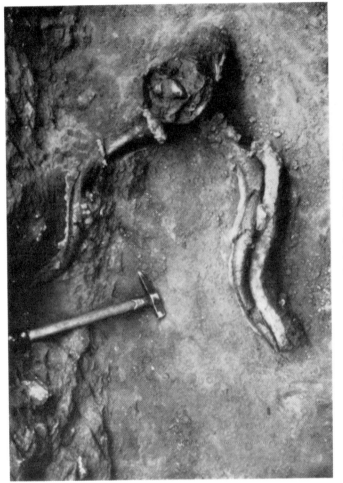

Fossil skull of a Kudu from Bed II at Oldoway.
(By permission of *Illustrated London News*)

period which we call Kamasian came to an end at about the same time as the final great faulting movements of the earth's crust which gave us the Rift Valley in its present form. The end of the Kamasian Pluvial period also marks the extinction of a very large number of the species which previously flourished in East Africa, and in the fossil beds of the next pluvial period we find a very different fauna which closely resembles that of present-day conditions. Why, we may ask, did some species suddenly become extinguished in the area while others managed to survive? So far as I can see the probable answer to this question is that the fauna of the district was largely exterminated by the change in climatic conditions, and that when at length a fresh wet period set in the area was reoccupied by animals from other regions which were not so seriously affected by the desiccation. It would seem on theoretical grounds, moreover, that in the area which thus served as a reservoir during the dry period, conditions were such that certain species did not live there. For example, we must suppose that in the hypothetical reservoir from which most of the modern East African mammals came, species such as *Hipparion*, *Pelorovis*, &c., did not occur.

Where was this reservoir, whence did these animals come back? Unfortunately, as I have already pointed out, we know as yet nothing of the prehistoric fauna of the great Congo-Nigeria region, which to-day harbours in the main a distinct fauna, but it seems more than likely that this region—which to-day is wetter than the East and South African zone—was not completely affected by the general desiccation of the interpluvial periods, and so may have been able to act as a 'reservoir' for species that were already living there and for species that managed to find their way there as the rest of the country dried up.

Among the very few species now extinct which are found in the deposits of the last pluvial period are a small bovine and a large water buffalo. The latter is of Asiatic type and presumably was also present in the previous wet period although its remains have not yet been identified for certain in these older beds in East Africa.

One of the chief differences between the fauna of the last part of the Pleistocene in East Africa and the fauna of the same period in North Africa is that the latter includes a greater percentage of extinct species as well as of species which no longer inhabit that region. This can be partly explained by the fact that the North African region was cut off from the 'reservoir' by the Saharan desert belt and that it was not until later, when the wet period had been in existence sufficiently long to allow animals gradually to work their way northward across the Sahara area once more, that the North African fauna was replenished from the south with typical African species, and partly by the fact that at this time North Africa was apparently deriving some of its fauna from the Near East.

We must turn next to South Africa—which is also a part of our third faunal region—and see what information is available from there concerning the fauna of the Pleistocene. Unfortunately, although the Stone Age period has been studied in South Africa far longer than in East Africa, there is still only very little knowledge about the fauna associated with Stone Age cultures there. Quite a number of extinct species of animals which obviously belong to the Pleistocene period have been found and recorded, but they have very rarely been found in circumstances which give any accurate information as to what part of the Pleistocene they represent, or with what stages of Stone Age culture they are associated.

Professor van Riet Lowe, head of the Bureau of

Archaeology at Johannesburg, has very kindly supplied me with some notes which he has given me permission to make use of in this book. To Professor Lowe, too, we owe the only fairly comprehensive attempt to list the various identified Pleistocene mammals reported from South Africa, and to show their approximate relationship with the Stone Age cultures. I have to use the word 'approximate' because in many cases the fossils and culture have not been found in proved association. In a few cases, however, notably at the Sheppard Island site excavated by Professor Lowe,[1] the association of fauna and culture stages has been proved.

In view of the uncertain nature of the relationships of the earlier faunas to the cultures in South Africa, all that can be safely said at present is that in the deposits of the earliest part of the Pleistocene—deposits which are now yielding evidence of the presence of a primitive pre-Chellean pebble culture—the extinct animals include a *Mastodon*, several very primitive elephants, a short-necked giraffid, and a large hippopotamus. In so far as this list goes, it compares closely with the fauna list of the same period—the earliest Pleistocene—both in East and North Africa.

In the rather later deposits which have yielded typical series of the great hand-axe culture, the Chelleo-Acheulean, the fauna list is rather more complete. The *Mastodon* is no longer present, the elephants are of a more evolved type, the zebra is present as well as a large horse, *Equus capensis*. Lion, leopard, and two species of hyaena represent the carnivores, a gigantic buffalo of Asiatic affinities is present, and there are also two species of rhinoceros. This list is very far from complete, but

---

[1] Recent work at River View Estates, Windsorton, has also yielded a fauna in direct association with human cultures (see later).

Professor Lowe tells me that recent excavations have
yielded a fauna including remains of extinct elephant,
hippopotamus, giraffe, pig, buffalo, and antelope, which,
however, have not yet been specifically identified. These
are very definitely associated with a late stage of the hand-
axe culture comparable to the Acheulean. At Sheppard
Island the remains of extinct elephants of the Archidiskodon group[1] were found in direct association with
a very late stage of the hand-axe culture.

As far, therefore, as the available evidence goes, we may
say that the fauna associated with the hand-axe culture in
South Africa has much the same elements as that of East
and North Africa.

In one particular, however, there is a very great difference, which needs confirmation before it is accepted as
finally proved. In the list of animals from the deposits
which yield the hand-axe culture there is one record of
the presence of the African elephant. If this is correct,
then it would seem that possibly South Africa was the
evolutionary home of the African elephant and that it
spread northwards from there at a much later date. This
idea received some support from the fact that some of
the earlier extinct South African elephants have been
regarded by one or two writers as possible, though not
certain, ancestors of the modern species.

Professor Lowe believes that there is evidence now that
after the time of the great hand-axe cultures, which
apparently had a wetter climate than at present, there was
a long arid period. The next period to which extinct
animals can definitely be assigned is a period of renewed

[1] In a paper in *Nature* in April 1928, p. 673, the late Prof. F. Osborn
reviewed the finds of fossil elephants in South Africa, and showed that
elephants found at Sheppard Island and other sites with the Upper
Stellenbosch culture are of evolved type and are comparable in age
with the *E. antiquus* of East Africa.

wet conditions. Here the fauna includes a very large equid, a large buffalo, and a number of ungulates. The culture stages of the Upper Pleistocene will be described in the appropriate chapter, but it may be said here that they seem to indicate a lagging behind as compared with the cultures farther north. This is in keeping with the geographical position, which is a cul-de-sac.

After this time nearly all the animals found in South Africa (i.e. in the deposits which represented the very final and closing stages of the Pleistocene) are of the same species as those living in Africa to-day. The important exceptions are the great water-buffalo and an extinct equid, which are also the important exceptions in East Africa.[1]

On the available evidence we may thus conclude that the South African fauna of the Pleistocene compares well with that of East Africa.

Before leaving South Africa a brief reference must be made to a very important fossil discovery which, however, cannot be related in any way to the Stone Age cultures. Late in 1924 an anthropoid skull was discovered at a place called Taungs. The age of the Taungs skull is still in dispute. By some scientists it is placed as Lower Pleistocene, by others as much earlier—Pliocene or even Miocene. Personally, I am inclined to believe that it is of Early Pleistocene date. The skull, which is of an immature animal, is that of an ape allied to the gorillas and chimpanzees but distinct from them in many ways. Its interest to us in this chapter is that it suggests that the fauna which now characterizes our second faunal region— the Congo and West Africa—was formerly far more

[1] In publications by T. F. Dreyer and A. Lyle of Grey University College and also by E. C. van Hoepen, a number of new species of animals from South Africa are described, but it is questionable whether many of them are more than local races of known living species.

widespread. The Taungs skull will be discussed in another chapter.

Before concluding this chapter on the fauna of the Stone Age in Africa, mention must be made of two other areas which have yielded faunal remains belonging to the Stone Age period. At Broken Hill in North Rhodesia the famous Broken Hill mine yielded an extensive fauna which was claimed to be associated with the skull from the same site. Although there is reason to believe that this association is not absolutely indisputable, it is worth recording that from the large dumps of cave material which were still available in 1929, I personally collected many fossils together with stone implements. The fossils represent a fauna in almost every detail similar to that of the present day, and the culture belongs to the same group which both in East Africa and in South Africa is associated with a modern fauna. This will be further discussed in other chapters, but it shows that the Rhodesian faunal evidence is in harmony with that of other areas. In the north of Nyasaland Dr. F. Dixey, the director of the Nyasaland Geological survey, found some deposits of early Pleistocene Age from which a few fragmentary fossils were obtained. These fossils have been examined by Dr. A. T. Hopwood, who records that they include remains of a *Mastodon* and a giraffid. Dr. Dixey submitted to me some very crude humanly flaked pebbles which were found on the surface, and apparently derived from the same bed, and some others have been given to me by Mr. Parrington. These tools represent undoubtedly a pre-Chellean pebble culture, so that once again we have the association of a *Mastodon* with this early stage of culture.

We may summarize the evidence outlined in this chapter as follows.

The earliest part of the Pleistocene in Africa has a fauna which includes archaic forms which have survived from the Pliocene as, for example, *Mastodon*, *Deinotherium*, and three-toed horses, and in addition it has true but primitive elephants, pigs, &c. (The human culture is very crude.)

The next part of the Pleistocene (Middle Pleistocene) has a fauna with many extinct species, but also includes many forms identical with those of the present day. The culture stage is that of the great hand-axe Chelleo-Acheulean complex. The final part of the Pleistocene proper, as well as the earlier part of the Holocene or Recent, has a fauna differing only a little from that of the present day; the most notable exceptions from the modern fauna being species of the Asiatic water-buffalo and an equid.

CHAPTER III

THE STONE AGE CULTURES OF EAST AFRICA

THE presence of prehistoric stone implements in East Africa was first recognized by the late Professor J. W. Gregory as far back as 1893, but no serious attempt to investigate the sequence of cultures was carried out until after the War, when Mr. E. J. Wayland, the newly-appointed Director of the Geological Survey of Uganda Protectorate, started to collect information and evidence upon this subject in the territory under his care.

In Kenya Colony and Tanganyika Territory detailed investigation was delayed still longer and was not seriously attempted in the former until 1926 and in the latter until 1931.

To-day the sequence of Stone Age cultures in this area is comparative well known, and since it is the part of Africa where I have made my personal studies I have decided to discuss the whole question from the East African aspect first of all and then to pass on to a review of the position in other parts of the continent.

As we have already seen in the preceding chapters both the climatic and geographical changes of the Pleistocene period, and also the fauna of the same period, are somewhat better known in East Africa than elsewhere, and that fact makes it easier for us to elucidate the whole story of the evolution of culture there than it is elsewhere in Africa.

When material representing the various cultures of the Stone Age is only found on the surface of the ground or in deposits which cannot be accurately dated, the exact sequence and the relative dating is very hard, if not impossible, to ascertain. In East Africa, however, except in so far as a few cultural stages are concerned, the cultures can be accurately placed in their relative chronological positions.

The earliest known and most primitive Stone Age culture in the East African region is that which Mr. E. J. Wayland has named the Kafuan. The implements, or rather artefacts, of this culture consist usually of a simple pebble from which one or two flakes have been struck in such a way that the intersection of the flake surfaces with the surface of the pebble give an irregular cutting edge.

This culture, in its earliest and most primitive form, has not as yet been found *in situ* in either Kenya or Tanganyika Territory so far as I am aware, although from surface finds its presence can be taken as certain. In the course of time the most simple pebble tool became slightly more developed, and in his latest published paper[1] Mr. Wayland shows in his table four distinct stages of the Kafuan culture which he designates Earliest Kafuan, Early Kafuan, Later Kafuan, and Developed Kafuan, respectively. From his paper it is not clear whether this fourfold division of the Kafuan culture is based upon a definite typological evolution, or whether it is simply a question of a Kafuan culture occurring in a series of four horizons each stratigraphically later than the preceding one.

Meanwhile, until fuller information is published, all that we need say is that during the earliest part of the Pleistocene—the true Lower Pleistocene—the Kafuan was the chief culture present, and that it persisted over a very long period with very little change. Following upon the Kafuan culture came a culture stage which Mr. Wayland calls pre-Chellean and to which I have given the name of the Oldowan culture. I should have preferred to call it 'Developed Kafuan', but Mr. Wayland holds that it is

[1] 'Rifts, Rivers, Rains, and Early Man in Uganda', *J.R.A.I.*, vol. lxiv, pp. 333 et seqq.

quite distinct from even the most developed Kafuan, and I have accepted his view until I can see the whole of his evidence and form my own opinion.

I suspect, however, that there is not really any justification for giving a separate culture name to the last stage of the 'pebble culture', and eventually the name 'Oldowan' will probably be dropped.

The Oldowan culture comprises a series of artefacts which are made either from water-worn pebbles or from lumps of rock. The piece of material to be made into a tool was then trimmed very roughly by striking off flakes in two directions so that the line of intersection of these flake scars gave a jagged cutting edge along one side of the pebble or lump of rock.

The type site of the Oldowan culture is the lowest bed (Bed I) of the series of alluvial deposits exposed in the Oldoway Gorge in Tanganyika Territory, and it is associated with a fauna which includes many archaic species of animals, but which also includes more evolved forms such as *Elephas antiquus*, the straight-tusked elephant. On the basis of this evidence the Oldowan pebble culture—which can be regarded as the final culmination of the evolution of the Kafuan pebble culture—can be regarded as belonging to the early part of the Middle Pleistocene period.

Both at Oldoway in Bed I and also, I believe, in Uganda there is some evidence which suggests that contemporary with the pebble culture (which, as we shall see presently, was the parent of the great hand-axe culture) there was another culture in which the artefacts were habitually made on flakes, but as yet there is insufficient information upon which to make any more definite statement about this early 'flake culture'.

The Oldoway Gorge, which has already been mentioned several times, exposes a series of strata with a total thickness of over 300 feet, and these beds have yielded a very valuable collection of stone implements which give us one of the most complete evolutionary sequence of stages of development of the Chelleo-Acheulean hand-axe culture that have been found. Altogether, eleven distinct evolutionary stages—each of which is both *typologically and stratigraphically* later than the preceding one—have been established and these will be the subject of a special monograph which is now in course of preparation.

The pebble-tools of the Oldowan culture, towards the top of Bed I, show a tendency to be trimmed in such a way as to leave a cutting edge on both sides, and in the lowest part of Bed II this tendency becomes a dominant character, and the trimming of two sides of a pebble leads to the making of very crude and simple hand-axes which I regard as representing the first true stage of the Chellean culture.

In the next stage the evolution goes one step farther and the type tools are rather large and clumsy pointed implements in which there is often a markedly flat side with a ridge or keel along the opposite side. In fact, not a few of the specimens which belong to stage 2 of the Chellean exhibit characters recalling the so-called 'rostro carinate' of East Anglia, with a flat 'ventral surface' and a keeled 'dorsal surface'.

In the third evolutionary stage the flat ventral surface is retained, but the dorsal keeling becomes much less marked. The implements become more shapely and suggest that more care was taken. In outline they assume a much more 'hand-axe' form.

In the fourth evolutionary stage we find that the flat under surface is beginning to give way, so that the section through the middle of the specimens becomes more or less bi-convex instead of being triangular or trapizoidal.

The bi-convexity is, however, seldom symmetrical, the lower surface being, in general, a much flatter arc than the upper.

The fifth stage of the Chellean is the final stage, after which there appears for the first time evidence of the Acheulean technique of flaking. In this fifth and final stage of the Chellean the typical implements are for the most part bi-convex in section, the bi-convexity being more or less symmetrical. The hand-axes are trimmed more or less all round the edge in many, but not all, cases, and the general *form* of the implements is an Acheulean one.

As the division between Chellean and Acheulean is purely one of convenience I have retained the term 'Chellean' in describing the phase and regarded it as the final Chellean rather than an early Acheulean, because the dominant *technique* is still Chellean although the *form* is Acheulean. There undoubtedly are prehistorians who, if faced with a series from this horizon, would describe it as early Acheulean (because of the form); the real fact of the matter is that it represents a transitional phase.

In the next horizon above that which yields this final Chellean (or transitional) we find that an absolutely unmistakable Acheulean technique is present although by no means all of the implements were made by this technique. This stage I term Acheulean 1.

This first stage of the Acheulean is also marked by the appearance for the first time (as far as the evidence at present available goes) of a type of implement which has not occurred before but which is a more or less common and typical tool in all the stages of the Acheulean. This implement is the cleaver.

Unlike *coups de poing* or hand-axes, the cleaver has at one end a comparatively straight axe-edge instead of a

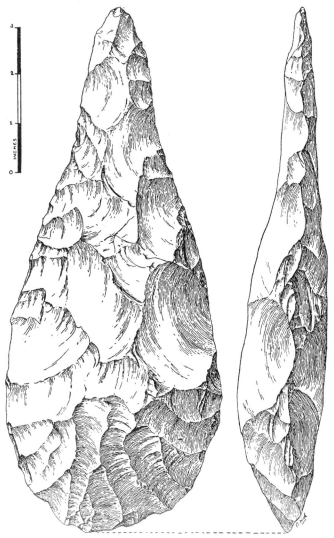

FIG. 2. Hand-axe of Acheulean stage 4 from Lewa, N. Kenya

pointed or rounded end. Although by no means as common in the Acheulean of Europe as it is in Africa, the cleaver is also a type tool of the European Acheulean.

After the first stage of the true Acheulean in the Oldoway sequence, cultural evolution was speeded up and in quick succession five further stages of the Acheulean are developed.

In the second stage fairly large pointed hand-axes dominate, but a few rather badly made 'ovates' appear. In the third stage ovates become common, the tendency is for the tools to be smaller and finer and the cleavers are many of them U-shaped.

Acheulean stage 4 is characterized by the presence of very large, exceedingly well-made pointed hand-axes, some of them going up to 13 and 14 inches in length. Very commonly these are asymmetrical in outline, while the section through the pointed ends is very, very thin.

In addition in the fourth stage of the Acheulean there are many almond-shaped hand-axes as well as a few ovates, while the dominant type of cleaver has a parallelogram section and is often square butted, i.e. rectangular in outline, although U-shaped specimens of the type found earlier occur.

In the next or fifth stage, the large-pointed hand-axes become exceedingly rare and instead we have a profusion of variations of the ovate and almond-shaped hand-axes, usually exhibiting a very high degree of skilful workmanship.

The fourth and fifth stages of the Acheulean mark the peak of workmanship and in Acheulean stage 6 there is a marked falling off, although an occasional specimen is as well-made as any in the two preceding stages. One or two of the cleavers of Acheulean stage 6 are of very remarkable beauty and surpass anything found earlier.

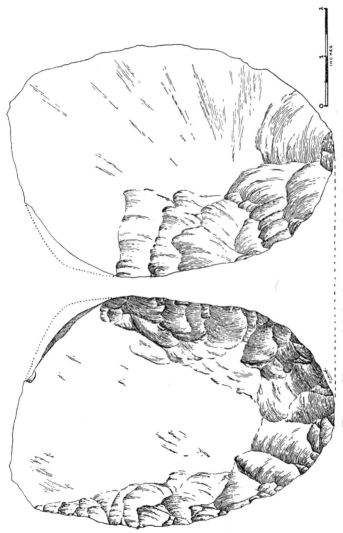

FIG. 3. Cleaver of Acheulean stage 4 from Lewa, N. Kenya

Although Oldoway is the site which has yielded the most complete evolutionary sequence of the stage of the hand-axe culture in East Africa, there are many sites in other parts of East Africa which have yielded material belonging to one or more of the stages. In Uganda Mr. Wayland has as yet unpublished sites where a sequence very nearly as complete can, I believe, be worked out. In Kenya, as long ago as 1913, an excellent collection of hand-axes was brought in to the Museum in Nairobi by a farmer, who was unfortunately killed in the War and whose secret of where he obtained the series perished with him. These specimens of Mr. Harrison's represent a very early stage of the Acheulean. From the Kariandusi River site found by Dr. J. Solomon and Miss E. Kitson when they were members of my second Expedition in 1928–9, I have described a series of hand-axes in my book, *The Stone Age Cultures of Kenya Colony*. In that book I stated that both a late Chellean and an Acheulean stage of the hand-axe culture was present at this site, but subsequent work has shown that in fact the Kariandusi River site was a factory site of the time of the fourth stage of the Acheulean. Implements that I formerly described as late Chellean are in fact merely unfinished specimens from the factory site. We now have a collection of over two thousand specimens excavated from an area barely 10 feet square, and the true explanation is clearly that given above.

One of the interesting things about this factory site is that apparently the craftsman or craftsmen who made use of this site confined themselves to the making of only a few of the hand-axe types which characterize Acheulean stage 4, and the long asymmetrical points are missing. I am nevertheless satisfied, from the big series which I have been able to examine, that the stage of culture represented is Acheulean 4.

North of Mount Kenya, at a site called Lewa, Mr. S. Howard located another very rich site of Acheulean stage 4, and this site has yielded some of the finest examples of the long asymmetrical type of hand-axe that I have ever seen, in addition to more normal specimens.

In the Kavirondo country which borders Victoria Nyanza to the north-east, Archdeacon Owen and others have made extensive collections of Stone Age material (some of which will be further mentioned in the next chapter) and this includes hand-axes of almost every stage of the Chelleo-Acheulean culture. Much of this material was, however, collected on the surface, while many of the specimens there found *in situ* were in unfossiliferous deposits which are as yet undated, except upon cultural evidence.

In an area on the southern shores of the Kavirondo Gulf between Kendu Bay and Homa Mountain there are fossiliferous deposits, some of which belong to the earliest part of the Pleistocene while others are of Middle Pleistocene Age. The former have yielded a few pebble tools and the latter implements of the late Chellean and early Acheulean types, but the area is not at all rich culturally.

The most easterly finds of hand-axes in East Africa are specimens collected on Mombasa Island by the late J. Rickman. The chief value of these undocumented specimens is that they show that the makers of the hand-axe culture spread right to the sea coast.

In Europe it has been established that the cultures known as Levalloisian and Clactonian were contemporary with the later stages of the great hand-axes or Chelleo-Acheulean culture, and a similar state of affairs is now also recognized for East Africa, although the published evidence is still very incomplete.

At the famous Oldoway Gorge a few typical examples

of implements made with a Levalloisian technique have
been found in the same horizons as those which yield
the later stages of the Acheulean culture, while elsewhere
in East Africa a similar association has been noticed. In
Uganda Mr. Wayland has identified a culture to which
he gives the name of Sangoan, which is the contemporary
of the Acheulean. His detailed study of this culture, as
well as of his other material, is eagerly awaited, but meanwhile it would appear from remarks in his latest publication that Mr. Wayland considers the Sangoan to be
mainly a flake culture allied to the Levalloisian but
influenced to some extent by elements of the hand-axe
culture. In his table published in 1934 he shows it as
being ancestral to the 'Mousterian' of Uganda.

In other parts of East Africa, most notably in the
Kericho-Sotik region of Kenya and in the Kavirondo
country bordering the Victoria Nyanza, much material of
a typically Levalloisian form occurs.

An assemblage from a site in South Kavirondo called
Ober Awach, first located by Archdeacon Owen—and
which I have subsequently visited on several occasions—
would appear to be identical to Mr. Wayland's Late Sangoan, but at Ober Awach there is no evidence upon which
the relative age of the culture can be ascertained. Quite
distinct from the Sangoan, however, are certain assemblages from various parts of Kenya which are in every
way typical of the true Levalloisian, and I have no hesitation in saying that I am convinced that before long we
shall have positive evidence that the later stages of the
hand-axe culture in East Africa were contemporary with
both a Sangoan culture and a true Levalloisian culture.

The closing stages of the Middle Pleistocene period
coincided with the end of the Kamasian Pluvial period,
and we have evidence that towards the end of this pluvial

period the former great lakes dwindled until there were but a few swamps on the floors of their basins. In the deposits formed at this time—deposits formed in these swamps—we find evidence of the contemporary existence of four distinct types of culture. The best sites where this evidence can be found are on the top of the Kinangop Plateau in Kenya, where these old swamp beds are well exposed and are rich in stone tools. It would appear as though members of the tribes or races making these various cultures gathered round these swampy areas as the climate became more arid and a number of distinct living sites have been found. At three of these a very curious culture, a derivative of the Levalloisian and yet with some evidence of Acheulean influence, occurs. This culture I have provisionally named a Pseudo-Stillbay because at first sight many of the tools suggest a Stillbay culture. I will describe this culture in brief presently. At the same horizon but not at the same sites, tools of the Nanyukian culture can be found. This culture I described in *The Stone Age Cultures of Kenya Colony* from a site on the slopes of Mount Kenya. At that time there was no positive evidence of the stratigraphical position of the Nanyukian, but on typological grounds it was placed as later than the Acheulean proper. This now has proved to be practically correct, but not quite, for the evidence from the Kinangop shows that the sixth and final stage of the Acheulean was contemporary with the Nanyukian and the Pseudo-Stillbay. The fourth culture which belongs to this period, the very close of the Kamasian Pluvial period, is a very crude stage of a true Aurignacian culture. This has as yet only been found *in situ* at one site in the Kinangop swamp deposits, but its presence is certain.

Having indicated what the four contemporary cultures

E

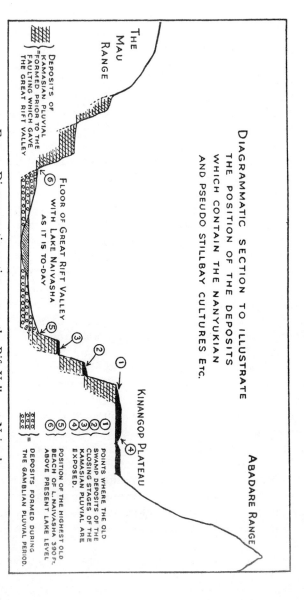

DIAGRAMMATIC SECTION TO ILLUSTRATE
THE POSITION OF THE DEPOSITS
WHICH CONTAIN THE NANYUKIAN
AND PSEUDO STILLBAY CULTURES ETC.

THE
MAU
RANGE

ABADARE RANGE

KINANGOP PLATEAU

FLOOR OF GREAT RIFT VALLEY
WITH LAKE NAIVASHA
AS IT IS TO-DAY

DEPOSITS OF
KAMASIAN PLUVIAL
=FORMED PRIOR TO THE
FAULTING WHICH GAVE
THE GREAT RIFT VALLEY

① ② ③ ④ = POINTS WHERE THE OLD
SWAMP DEPOSITS OF THE
CLOSING STAGES OF THE
KAMASIAN PLUVIAL ARE
EXPOSED.

⑤ = POSITION OF THE HIGHEST OLD
BEACH OF L. NAIVASHA 390 FT.
ABOVE PRESENT LAKE LEVEL

⑥ = DEPOSITS FORMED DURING
THE GAMBLIAN PLUVIAL PERIOD.

Fig. 4. Diagrammatic section across the Rift Valley at Naivasha

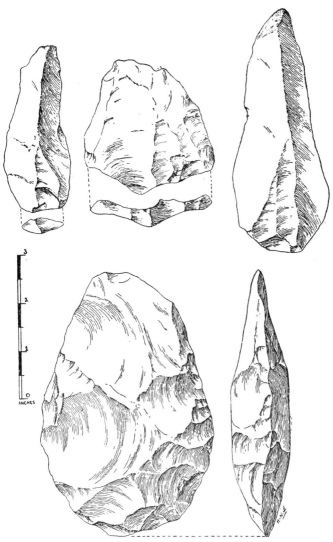

FIG. 5. Typical hand-axe and flakes of the Nanyukian culture
from Kinangop Plateau site and Nanyuki

were, let me describe in more detail the implements which are typical of them.

The Pseudo-Stillbay is characterized by very small pointed implements of which there are two main groups. One group has the secondary flaking only on the upper surface; and, in fact, the implements of this group are typologically simply very small 'Mousterian points'. The other group consists of implements worked all over both faces and the main bulbs of percussion trimmed away, leaving what may be described as a minute *coup de poing* of triangular shape. It is from the presence of this second group that the name Pseudo-Stillbay is derived. Superficially, these little implements very strongly recall Stillbay points, but in fact the technique employed in carrying out the secondary trimming is quite distinct, so that any careful scrutiny soon reveals that they are not really of Stillbay type at all.

As this culture has not yet been published with illustrations, but only recorded, I am illustrating it with drawings of a series of specimens in this chapter and for contrasts am showing a few typical Stillbay types.

This Pseudo-Stillbay culture is, as I have already said, by no means confined to the Kinangop Plateau although the best sites known to me are there. It occurs *in situ* elsewhere in Kenya, while in Uganda Mr. Wayland has found it in stratigraphically the same position, that is to say, at the very end of the period covered by the evolution of the Acheulean culture.

The Pseudo-Stillbay culture is best regarded as a branch derivative of the Levalloisian, influenced by the Acheulean, and the Nanyukian also has the same parentage, but a slightly different hybrid has been the result in this case. The type tools consist of well-made hand-axes of medium

FIG. 6. *Top row*: Basal Aurignacian from the Kinangop Plateau site contemporary with Nanyukian and the Pseudo-Stillbay. *The remainder* are implements of the Pseudo-Stillbay from the same deposits: contrast with fig. 7, p. 64.

size and commonly of very triangular form, with a very thin section, very well made small cleavers, and in addition flakes, points, and side scrapers of pure Levalloisian form.

The Nanyukian is, in fact, very nearly an exact counterpart of the Fauresmith culture of South Africa which we shall discuss in Chapter V. So far as I am aware the Nanyukian culture has only been found in two areas in Kenya—in the swamp deposits which mark the final stages of the Kamasian pluvial decline and on the slopes of Mount Kenya at an altitude of about seven to eight thousand feet. The later position is also suggestive of the fact that the climate of the country was at the time getting dry and hot and that water was scarce, for the slopes of a high snow-capped mountain like Kenya would have streams long after the water supply in lower country had dried up, as is evidenced by what happens in periods of severe drought in that country to-day.

The implements of the final stage of the Acheulean found at this time differ in no way from those of the final stage of the Acheulean at Oldoway and elsewhere, and need no further description.

The tools of the earliest yet recognized stage of the Aurignacian culture in East Africa which is, as we have seen, contemporary with these other three, are only represented by a very small collection from a site on Mr. Cartwright's farm on the Kinangop. A series is illustrated. It includes a few crude 'backed blades' or knives, with blunted backs, a few true burins or chisels, and some crude scrapers.

At present we have no direct evidence as to the parentage of the East African Aurignacian culture, which later grew and developed into a most perfect expression of this widespread culture complex.

I have always believed that it is highly probable that

the Aurignacian was derived from the Acheulean culture. In the Kericho-Sotik area of Kenya Dr. J. D. Solomon, while a member of my 1928-9 Expedition, found a surface site from which he collected a very interesting assemblage of implements. It is highly unfortunate that these were only a surface find and that their age is so uncertain, because from a typological point of view they represent exactly the sort of assemblage that I have long expected as a link between the late Acheulean and the early Aurignacian. It is very much to be hoped that before many years are passed a similar assemblage will be found under more satisfactory conditions, so that this point can be settled.

In the table which follows I have set out the culture sequence of East Africa, as far as we know it at present, for the Lower and Middle parts of the Pleistocene period.

Although it is thus seen that we know a great deal about the Stone Age of East Africa at this time, it would be foolish to imagine that there is not still a great deal to be found out and many points to be elucidated.

Possibly further discoveries will necessitate some measure of revision as well as much amplification, but only so can progress be achieved. In the next chapter the story of the later Stone Age cultures, which belong to the Upper Pleistocene and the early part of recent times, will be told and the account of the East African sequence, as at present known, will be completed.

TABLE OF THE CULTURES OF THE LOWER AND MIDDLE PLEISTOCENE

End of Kamasian Pluvial = End of Middle Pleistocene

Acheulean 6	Early Aurignacian	Pseudo-Stillbay	Nanyukian
5	Proto Aurignacian?		
4		Sangoan	Early Levalloisian
3			
2			
Acheulean 1			
Chellean 5 or Transitional		Early Sangoan	
4			
3			
2			
Chellean 1			
Oldowan or pre-Chellean			
	End of Lower Pleistocene		
Developed Kafuan		Traces of a crude flake culture	
Earliest Kafuan			

End of Pliocene and beginning of Pleistocene

Note. Since writing this chapter a short article has been published in *Man* in which Mr. P. O'Brien suggests certain ideas in connexion with the Stone Age cultures of Uganda. Among other things he suggests that an early stage of the Tumbian culture was contemporary with the Late Acheulean, but we must wait to see what proof of this he has found before accepting it.

CHAPTER IV

THE STONE AGE CULTURES OF
EAST AFRICA (*cont.*)

IN the last chapter I summarized the sequence of Stone Age cultures which occur in East Africa in the deposits which are attributable on geological and paleontological grounds to the Lower and Middle Pleistocene.

As we saw in Chapter I, the close of the Middle Pleistocene period was marked by earth movements of great severity which resulted in the formation of the eastern branch of the Rift Valley as we know it to-day. We have no exact knowledge of what happened during this period of earth movements, except that we know that the desiccation—which had already resulted in the reduction of great lakes into small swampy areas—continued. We also know that a high percentage of the species of animals living in Kamasian times died out.

Subsequently the climate became more humid once again and the rainfall apparently exceeded that of the present day, for the level of the lakes in the basins on the floor of the Great Rift Valley rose very considerably, attaining—in the case of some of the smaller basins—to levels as much as 700 and 500 feet above the present-day level of the water in these same basins.

The sequence of cultures which we are going to consider in this chapter start at the beginning of this new wet period, which we call the Gamblian Pluvial.[1] The story covers the whole Gamblian Pluvial period and carries over the

---

[1] Mr. Wayland does not agree that there was an arid period between the Kamasian and the Gamblian and holds that the Gamblian is simply a late phase of the Kamasian. My detailed objections to this view will be published shortly.

dry period which followed it. It continues in the short and less humid Makalian wet phase which marks the end of the Pleistocene and the beginning of the Holocene, and it ends in the period of the Nakuran wet phase, which belongs definitely to Recent or Holocene times.

At the close of the Kamasian Pluvial period there were present four distinct cultures, and possibly five, for I think that undoubtedly a pure Levalloisian was also present, although this remains to be proved. When the Gamblian Pluvial period started there were present, so far as our available evidence goes, only two quite distinct cultures, the Aurignacian and the Levalloisian, which by this time was very highly evolved. These two cultures were absolutely contemporaneous in East Africa at this time and developed independently side by side, often in the same area.

I have already published in *The Stone Age Cultures of Kenya Colony* an account of this parallel evolution, but in that book I wrongly used the term 'Lower Mousterian' to describe the developed Levalloisian, while I used the term 'Upper Mousterian' to describe the next stage of development of the Levalloisian. For this latter, in the light of the much more detailed evidence available to-day, I prefer the term 'Proto-Stillbay'.

The type stations where the parallel evolution was first studied and worked out were the Malewa Gorge near Naivasha, and the exposures on the banks of the Little Gilgil River, also in the Naivasha basin. Both these sections admirably expose the old lake beds laid down during the Gamblian Pluvial period, while the former also exhibits a terrace of the Makalian wet phase. The more detailed subdivision of the later part of the Aurignacian culture during the decline of the Gamblian Pluvial period was studied at the cave site on Mr. Gamble's farm at

Elmenteita in the Nakuru lake basin, and a full report of
the excavation of that site has been prepared for publication, in addition to the more general report which was
given in my book mentioned above.

From our earlier work it became abundantly evident
that towards the very end of the Gamblian Pluvial period
and during the succeeding dry period the culture stage,
which I formerly described as Upper Mousterian and
now call Proto-Stillbay, had been replaced by a stage in
which the assemblage of implements was in every way
comparable to that already described from South Africa
as the Stillbay culture.

Since the publication of my book we have carried out
excavations (in 1932) at a site called Apis Rock in the
northern part of Tanganyika Territory, which has given
us a very much deeper insight into the evolutionary
sequence which resulted in the Kenya form of the Stillbay
culture. We also now have several sites which have yielded
a much more complete series of implements representing
the final stage of the Upper Kenya Aurignacian, i.e.
phase c.

First of all let us briefly examine the evolution of the
Aurignacian culture from the beginning of the Gamblian
Pluvial period to its close, and then do likewise for the
developed Levalloisian and its derivatives.

As we have seen, the Aurignacian was already present
in the last stages of the decline of the Kamasian Pluvial
period, and the evidence available suggests that at first
there was no rapid evolution or development, for the
material representing the Aurignacian culture during the
first part of the Gamblian Pluvial period does not exhibit
any noticeably new features.

Towards the middle part of the Gamblian Pluvial
period a marked change occurs. The culture becomes

more virile and is characterized by the presence of very large numbers of backed blades often very well made, and by the tendency to make also many small crescent-shaped artefacts which are known as lunates. These lunates were apparently used as barbs for arrows, and possibly also for spears. From this, the first stage of what I have termed the Upper or Developed Kenya Aurignacian, there is a steady evolution, and in the second stage (phase b) the Aurignacian culture of East Africa reaches its zenith. The very greatest skill in workmanship is exhibited in the tools which often are really beautiful and very delicately worked. The third phase shows that degeneration has set in. The tools are often very roughly made although a proportion are still very beautiful.

Throughout the Upper Aurignacian the type tools are knife blades with blunted backs, burins (or chisels), round ended skin scrapers, sinew frayers, and triangular fabricators. Beads carved from ostrich egg-shell were commonly made, and bone splinters were sometimes polished into rough awls. There is also evidence that the people who made the Aurignacian culture were employing clay to line the insides of baskets in order to make them waterproof, and it is not unlikely that the actual making of pottery was thus invented. From Gamble's Cave and one or two other sites, small fragments of what can only be described as pottery have been found, but it is possible that they only represent the remains of clay-lined baskets that were accidentally burnt. Whether that is so or not, the presence of very good pots in the Elmenteitan culture —which later evolved from the Upper Aurignacian— suggests strongly that the lining of baskets with clay by the makers of the Upper Aurignacian culture led to the invention of pottery in this area.

The final stage of the Upper Aurignacian of East

Africa, phase c, was first found in Gamble's Cave, Elmenteita, where the evidence suggested that it belonged in time to the very end of the Gamblian Pluvial period. This view has been supported by more recent discoveries, among which special mention may be made of an assemblage of tools of this period found in the Oldoway Gorge in a geological position which shows that they just antedated the arid period which marks the end of the Gamblian Pluvial. Incidentally, this discovery at Oldoway is the most southerly find of the East African Aurignacian yet recorded.

At present in East Africa there is no direct evidence which associates the East African Aurignacian with any art, although it would seem highly probable from what we know in other parts of the world that the Aurignacians were artistic. As we shall see in a later chapter, there is a good deal of primitive Stone Age art in certain parts of East Africa, and it is to be hoped that future work will enable some direct link between the various culture stages and the art to be established.

Turning next to the evolution of the Upper Levalloisian and its derivatives, we have already seen that during the Kamasian Pluvial period—contemporary with the Acheulean stages of the hand-axe culture—there was present in East Africa a Levalloisian type of culture of which the Sangoan of Uganda and West Kenya is probably a specialized branch. Although there is no direct evidence of the pure Levalloisian in the very final stages of the Kamasian, we cannot do otherwise than assume its presence at that time because there is no doubt at all that it was present in East Africa earlier and also that at the beginning of the Gamblian Pluvial a developed Levalloisian was very widespread all over East Africa. Although the type station is at Naivasha in Central Kenya,

assemblages of tools belonging to the developed Levalloisian have been found as far east as Mombasa Island on
the coast, as well as over most of Kenya Colony and Uganda.
In Tanganyika Territory no finds are recorded, as far as
I know, farther south than the Oldoway region, but that
is solely because the central and southern parts of Tanganyika have yet to be the subject of a detailed prehistoric
survey.

The developed Levalloisian which is characterized by
a typical flake culture, with points and side scrapers made
on flakes struck from the type of core known as a 'tortoise
core', was, as we have seen, contemporary with the Lower
Aurignacian of East Africa. At first it seems to have
remained unaffected by the close proximity of this other
and very distinct culture, but towards the middle of the
Gamblian Pluvial period the developed Levalloisian was
influenced by the Aurignacian. The resultant stage of
culture which I formerly called Upper Kenya Mousterian
is characterized by two things. There is a very marked
tendency for the secondary trimming of the 'points' to
be extended over both faces of the implement, and also
it is noticeable that tool types such as the Aurignacian
backed blade are being copied. This latter point was not
clear when I wrote *The Stone Age Cultures of Kenya
Colony*, but becomes evident from a study of the material
which we excavated from the different occupational levels
of the shelter at Apis Rock in North Tanganyika. There,
in the lowest occupational horizons we have a pure and
simple developed Levalloisian. Next comes a level which
yielded very many implements of the type which I would
formerly have called 'Upper Mousterian'. Associated with
these are a *few* 'backed blades' and end scrapers, types of
tool borrowed from the Aurignacian culture as a result
of the contact. In this level there are also a number of

specimens on which, as I have said, the secondary trimming is extended over both faces of the 'points', and immediately above this occupational level is another, which yielded a typical Stillbay stage of culture.

In consequence, I now propose to substitute the name of Proto-Stillbay for Upper Kenya Mousterian to describe this Levalloisian development in the direction of the Stillbay.

The evolution of culture at Apis Rock is shown by a series of pages of drawings in·this chapter, and these perhaps show the evolution even better than any verbal description. The true Kenya Stillbay culture was first described by me from sites in the Nakuru-Naivasha region. It belongs in time to the very close of the Gamblian Pluvial period and continues on into the succeeding dry period. The most typical implements consist of very delicately worked points, and leaf-shaped blades and 'lozenges', all of which exhibit very beautiful pressure flaking which is comparable to, though by no means identical with, that found on Solutrean leaf-shaped tools in south-western Europe. The Stillbay stage of culture is also characterized by the presence of lunates, backed blades, and scrapers—types borrowed from the Aurignacian—and beads also occur. There is some evidence, as yet not wholly proved however, that in the latter part of the Stillbay stage of culture crude pottery was made. Sites of the true Stillbay culture occur over a widespread area in East Africa, although there is at present no record from the coastal region or from Central and South Tanganyika.

As I have already said, there is a superficial resemblance between some of the tools of the much earlier Pseudo-Stillbay stage of culture, and those of the true Stillbay. This resemblance is liable to be misleading unless the

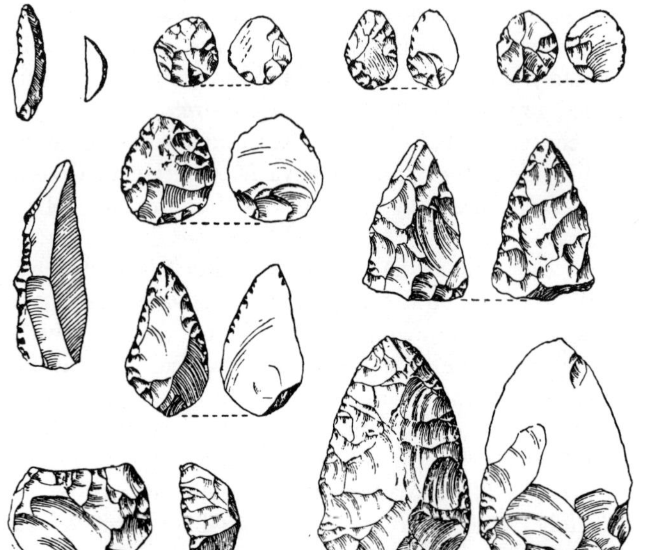

FIG. 7. *Above scale*, typical series of implements of the Kenya Stillbay culture from Apis Rock and Gilgil River. *Below scale*, typical series of Proto-Stillbay from Apis Rock

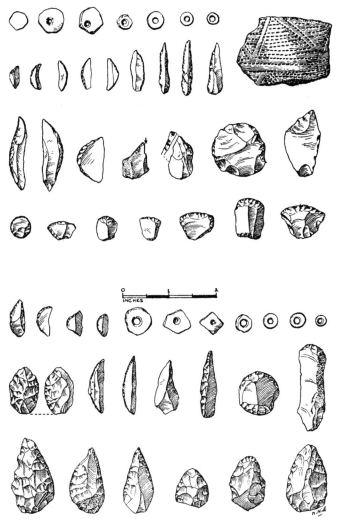

FIG. 8. *Above scale*, typical series of Kenya Wilton B. from Apis Rock. *Below scale*, typical series of Magosian from Apis Rock

F

difference in flaking technique is carefully studied. If a large series of tools is available and not single specimens, there should be no difficulty in deciding whether Pseudo-Stillbay or Stillbay proper is represented, because in the later, in a really representative series, the presence of backed blades and lunates will be an additional guide.

In 1926 Mr. E. J. Wayland of Uganda carried out an excavation at a site called Magosi in Karamoja, Uganda. Here he found a 'microlithic culture with a Stillbay flavour'. This I had the privilege of examining in 1927, and the collection was subsequently described in a paper by Mr. M. C. Burkitt and Mr. Wayland in 1932.[1]

The evidence collected by Mr. Wayland showed that this culture stage belonged to a post-pluvial dry period equated with that which followed the Gamblian Pluvial period and preceded the Makalian wet phase. Up to 1932 the Magosian culture had not, so far as I know, been found *in situ* anywhere except at the type site, but in 1932 when we were excavating at Apis Rock we found that a typical Magosian stage of culture followed immediately upon the Stillbay one and was undoubtedly derived from it.

Thus the Apis Rock evidence supports Mr. Wayland's view that the Magosian is derived from the Stillbay culture—with a microlithic element predominating—and that it belongs in time to the dry period following the close of the Gamblian Pluvial period. It lasted, however, for some time (a subdivision of the Magosian may one day be necessary) and continued on into the Makalian wet phase. This conclusion is drawn from the evidence at Apis Rock, where water conditions are such that during the arid period man could not have lived there at all.

It seems probable to me that the Magosian of Apis Rock

[1] 'The Magosian Culture of Uganda', *J.R.A.I.*, vol. lxii, 1932.

is of a slightly later date than that of Magosi itself, in fact, is an Upper Magosian, for at Apis Rock this culture is associated with pottery, while at Magosi itself no pottery occurred. Incidentally, it may be pointed out here that the Elmenteitan culture, which also belongs to the Makalian wet phase, had good pottery.

So far in East Africa the only cultural stages that can be unhesitatingly assigned to the dry period which followed the Gamblian Pluvial period are the evolved Stillbay and the Magosian, which is a derivative of the Stillbay and really can almost be regarded as a contemporary of the evolved Stillbay.

During the succeeding wet phase, the Makalian, we have already seen that the Magosian continued to develop, and contemporary with it was the Elmenteitan culture. The type station for the Elmenteitan culture is Gamble's Cave, Elmenteita, where an excellent representative assemblage was found in the uppermost prehistoric occupation level represented in the section. The Elmenteitan culture is a direct derivative of the Aurignacian and shows no trace at all of any influences from the Levalloisian-Stillbay element.

The chief ways in which the Elmenteitan differs from the Aurignacian are the following:

1. Long two-edged blades (often with the bulbs trimmed away to facilitate hafting) were used as knives (apparently with handles) instead of the Aurignacian 'backed blades', although a few of these are still found.

2. The principal fabricators of the Elmenteitan culture are what are known as *lames écaillées* instead of the triangular section fabricators of the Aurignacian.

3. Decorated pottery occurs in quantity. It is hand-made and the larger pots have conical bases and not

rounded bases. Small bowls are round bottomed, and there are traces of small flat-bottomed vessels, but of these a complete specimen has yet to be found.

The similarities between the Aurignacian and the El-menteitan are the presence of crescents or lunates, end scrapers, burins (which are not, however, very common), and bone awls.

The only occupational sites of the Elmenteitan culture as yet known are cave or rock-shelter sites, but scattered specimens attributable to the culture are found occasionally in the open. The distribution of the Elmenteitan culture is not yet well known. I have found traces of it over a large part of the highlands of Kenya and in the region on the north-east of Victoria Nyanza. When more excavations of caves and shelters are carried out I believe that it will be found to be fairly widespread.

Also belonging in time to the Makalian wet phase[1] we have two different branches of the Wilton culture. One of these—Wilton A—is characterized by the presence of very large numbers of very small double-ended 'thumb-nail' scrapers associated with numerous crescents, as well as a heterogenous collection of rather larger scrapers and a few burins and fabricators of the *lame écaillée* type.

Wilton A is found mainly in open station sites, although it does also seem to occur in some rock shelters. Wilton B, on the other hand, has so far only been found in rock shelters. It is a direct derivative of the Magosian, and although it has much in common with Wilton A—as, for example, thumb-nail scrapers and crescents—it is differentiated from it by having small degenerate points of the Stillbay type, thus betraying its origin in the Stillbay Magosian evolutionary sequence. I have found Wilton B both at Apis Rock in Tanganyika Territory—where it

[1] Wilton B continues on into the Nakuran wet phase.

follows immediately upon the developed Magosian—and at two small shelters in the Kabete district near Nairobi. In his table Mr. Wayland places the Wilton of Uganda as a direct derivative of the Magosian, so that I presume that he is referring to what I term Wilton B. I am certain, however, that Wilton A also extends into Uganda, as I have found sites within a few miles of the border in North Kavirondo country.

There is a third branch of the Wilton culture which at present cannot be accurately dated. It is found over a wide area along the shores of East African lakes, and it is always associated with immense shell-mounds or 'escargatoires'. In this branch of the Wilton, thumb-nail scrapers are very rare indeed, and the pottery is much coarser and quite different from that of Wilton A or B.

Excavations of two of these shell-mounds have been carried out, and it was found that stone tools of any kind were very rare, presumably because a diet which was almost exclusively of mollusca and fish did not require much in the way of weapons or implements. Beads are, however, common.

It is probable that the shell-mound branch of the Wilton which I term Wilton C started at about the same time as Wilton A and B and continued until much later, when the two had given way to the various branches of the Neolithic culture. This, however, is not yet firmly established.

The Makalian wet phase was followed by a short dry spell, when the levels of the smaller lakes dropped very considerably, and then came the Nakuran wet phase, which can be approximately dated as reaching its maximum about 1000–850 B.C.

The Nakuran wet phase resulted in a marked fresh rise in lake levels in those basins where there was no outlet, and there is abundant evidence that at this time the Stone

Age people of East Africa had reached a true Neolithic stage of culture.

Of the five distinct divisions of the Neolithic culture in East Africa, only two can at present be *proved* to belong to the Nakuran wet phase, although there is much indirect evidence which justifies assigning the other three to the same period.

The Gumban culture, which has two distinct branches, Gumban A and Gumban B, quite definitely belongs to the Nakuran wet phase. The culture of Gumban B is better known than that of Gumban A and it has a microlithic industry very similar indeed to Wilton A, and differs from the Wilton A chiefly in having beautifully made stone bowls, pestles and mortars, saddle-querns, and pottery with a rolled cord decoration and lugs. Associated with the Gumban A culture imported chalcedony, agate, and faience beads are found, of apparently Egyptian or other origin, as well as glass beads of Tel-el-Amarna type. Traces of imported iron also occur, but there is no evidence that either the metal or the beads were locally made, and I believe, therefore, that 'Neolithic' rather than 'Iron Age' is the best label for the Gumban culture. In time, *circa* 850 B.C. and later, it was certainly contemporary with the Metal Age in the Mediterranean basin. Presumably traders from the north, either from the Sudan or Abyssinia, were coming to East Africa for ivory and even perhaps for gold, and were bringing beads and metal for exchange with the Stone Age inhabitants.

The 'A' branch of the Gumban culture has a similar assemblage of artefacts, and occasionally also imported objects, but the pottery is very distinctive indeed, while the stone bowls tend to be flatter and more like plates.

The Gumban A pottery is characterized by a very curious deep scoring or scratching all over the interior surface of a high proportion of the pots *but not all* of them. This scoring was done before the pots were baked. So far no parallel for this has been traced in any other pottery anywhere in the world, and the reason remains obscure. Very often the pots of the A branch of the Gumban culture had the whole of the external surface decorated to represent a basket. Gumban A pottery has been illustrated in my book, *The Stone Age Cultures of Kenya Colony.*

Another difference between the A and the B branches of the Gumban culture lies in the method of burial. This will be discussed in Chapter IX.

Apparently only one of the East African Neolithic groups has polished axes. I have provisionally named this the Njoroan culture, but very little is known about it. Only about fifteen polished axes have so far been found, and their range is from the coast to Uganda. Microlithic industries are associated with them in some cases. At only one site was there any quantity of associated material, and that was at Njoro, where the axes were with crescents and scrapers and pottery, and were found in full-length burial trenches.

I have already indicated my belief that Wilton C continued into the Nakuran wet phase and was contemporary with the Neolithic stages, so that only one other Neolithic branch remains to be discussed.

From the Congo Dr. Jacques has described a large series of implements excavated by M. Hass at Tumba. The assemblage included a few polished axes, a very large number of arrow-heads of several types, leaf-shaped lance-heads, and a number of rather curious implements, some of them recalling Neolithic 'picks' in shape, and others recalling late Acheulean hand-axes in form but not technique. To this assemblage he has given the name of

the Tumbian culture, and it is necessary to record that
in East Africa, especially in Uganda and the western part
of Kenya, many surface finds seem to belong unquestion-
ably to this Tumbian. The polished axes and arrow-heads
found with the typical Tumbian culture place it definitely
in the Neolithic group, and I am confident that the Tumbian was present in East Africa at about the same time as
the Gumban. It is, incidentally, very noticeable that, so
far as our present limited knowledge goes, the true Gumban is not found at all in the areas where the material of
Tumbian affinities is being found. The relation of the
Tumbian to the Njoroan is much more problematical.
The polished axes so far found in Kenya (with possibly
two exceptions) are not of the Congo type at all, but recall
strongly stone axes from the Sudan, and I believe that
it is likely that the Tumbian and Njoroan branches of the
Neolithic culture will be found to be quite distinct when
further evidence is obtained, and I have consequently not
put them together.[1]

With the Neolithic stage of culture we come to an end
of the story of the Stone Age in East Africa, but in conclusion the warning must be given that the use of stone
for occasional implements continued for a very long time
indeed in East Africa. In some cases tribes using metal,
and knowing how to make it, still made occasional stone
tools, and in at least one or two cases there is evidence
to suggest that tribes having no knowledge of any other
than stone tools were living until only a few hundred
years ago, or less. Many of the Kenya tribes have a
tradition of a dwarf people who lived in holes or depressions in the ground and who are supposed to have been
finally exterminated only a hundred or so years ago. I

[1] *See* Note at end of Chapter III concerning possible early date for
some of the Tumbian material.

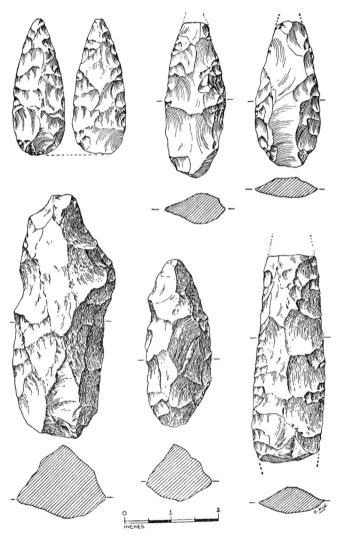

INCHES.

FIG. 9. Implements of the Tumbian culture from West Kenya
(compare with Fig. 19)

have excavated two of the depressions pointed out to me by old men as the places where their fathers told them these dwarfs lived, and in each case have found very thick coarse pottery, beads made of the seeds of wild bananas, and a few pieces of obsidian and chert flakes with a few scrapers and crescents. These dwarf people may well have been small local bands of Bushmen.

In Tanganyika Territory there is a little-known tribe living in the Eyassi region, which is said to speak a Bushman language with clicks, and who probably were using stone tools until a short time ago. More information about these people is badly needed.

The following table repeats that given at the end of Chapter III and completes it by adding the Stone Age culture stages of the Upper Pleistocene and Recent times in East Africa, so far as we know them at present.

NAKURAN WET PHASE	Gumban A	Gumban B	Njoroan	Tumbian	Wilton C
DRY					
MAKALIAN WET PHASE*	Elmenteitan		Wilton A	Wilton B Upper Magosian	
DRY			Late Stillbay	Lower Magosian	
GAMBLIAN PLUVIAL	Upper Aurignacian *c* Upper Aurignacian *b* Upper Aurignacian *a* Lower Aurignacian			Lower Stillbay Proto-Stillbay Levalloisian	
DRY	End of Middle Pleistocene (Marked by great earth movements and faulting)				
KAMASIAN PLUVIAL	Acheulean 6 Basal Aurignacian Acheulean 5 Proto-Aurignacian? Acheulean 4 Acheulean 3 Acheulean 2 Acheulean 1 Chellean 5 (or Transitional) Chellean 4 Chellean 3 Chellean 2 Chellean 1 Oldowan or pre-Chellean		Pseudo-Stillbay Sangoan Early Sangoan Traces of a flake culture	Nanyukian Levalloisian Early Levalloisian	
DRY?	End of Lower Pleistocene				
FIRST PLUVIAL	Developed Kafuan Earliest Kafuan		Traces of a flake culture		
DRY	End of Pliocene				

* Pleistocene ends and Holocene starts here.

CHAPTER V

THE STONE AGE CULTURES OF SOUTH AFRICA

IN this chapter I propose to summarize briefly the present state of our knowledge of the sequence of Stone Age cultures in South Africa.

The study of stone implements in South Africa dates from a very early period, and according to A. J. H. Goodwin, who has recently edited a paper summarizing the history of South African Prehistory and the present position,[1] the first South African antiquary was Colonel T. H. Bowker, who in 1855 had presented spear- or arrow-heads from 18 feet below the surface to the Museum in Capetown.

From that date onwards reports of finds of Stone Age implements become more and more numerous, and in the report mentioned above Mr. Goodwin and his colleagues have compiled and published a bibliography which comprises over two hundred published papers or books dealing with the Stone Age in South Africa.

In spite of this fact and in spite, too, of the fact that several leading European Prehistorians have in recent years visited South Africa in order to help elucidate the sequence of cultures and their inter-relationship, the head of the Bureau of Archaeology for the Union of South Africa had to write in reply to my request for information to be incorporated in this chapter, 'We know aggravatingly little'. This referred not so much to the Stone Age implements or even the cultures of South Africa, but to the far more important question of their exact relationship to each other and to changes of climate and extinct faunas, without which knowledge comparison with other parts of the world is of very little value.

[1] *Bantu Studies*, 1935 (see bibliography).

Geographically speaking South Africa is a cul-de-sac, and that is one of the things which lies at the root of all the difficulties and problems in connexion with the elucidation of the Stone Age of South Africa. The other thing is that in South Africa, until very recently indeed, a very high percentage of those who were interested in the Stone Age were mere collectors of specimens and not scientists really concerned with the problems of the age of the cultures.

The proper study of the past can only be carried out if prehistorians work in close co-operation with geologists and palaeontologists. To-day this is being done in South Africa and the prospects for the future are bright, although it must be said at once that the problems to be solved are in many cases highly complex because of the fact of the region being a cul-de-sac. So far as the earlier part of the Pleistocene was concerned this did not matter so much, but as time went on wave after wave of migration into the area complicated things exceedingly, as we shall see.

Before I proceed to summarize the sequence in South Africa, as I interpret it, I must draw attention to certain other important summaries which have been made in the last eight years.

In 1928 Mr. M. C. Burkitt, lecturer in Prehistory at the University of Cambridge, published a book called *South African Past in Stone and Paint*, and this was closely followed by a publication by A. J. H. Goodwin and C. van Riet Lowe entitled *The Stone Age Cultures of South Africa*. In 1930 Professor Breuil of the Collège de France published a brief summary of the position as he saw it after a visit of eleven weeks in 1929. This paper appeared in *L'Anthropologie*, vol. xl. In 1931 the same author published a review of the Stone Age in Africa as a whole under the title of 'L'Afrique Préhistorique'. This study appeared in a journal devoted in the ordinary way solely to art, and is consequently very little known. In it Professor Breuil again summarized the Stone Age cultures of South Africa as he interpreted them. Finally, in 1935, in the publication already mentioned, after summarizing the history of prehistory in South Africa, A. J. H. Goodwin gives a short summary of 'The present position of South African Prehistory'.

While I have naturally consulted the works of all of these authorities upon questions of fact, I do not wish to pretend to follow them of necessity in matters of interpretation, which I base upon my own knowledge of the position in East Africa and upon a close study of collections, both in South Africa and in this country.

Professor van Riet Lowe, the head of the Bureau of Archaeology, has very kindly put at my disposal the following table summarizing the position, and I shall use it as the basis of my own remarks. He has also kindly sent me a long typescript note with much valuable recent information, which I very gratefully acknowledge.

Culture Groups.	Climate.
Later Stone Age	Present-day conditions.
Middle Stone Age Complex	Wet?
. . . .	An arid period.
Upper Fauresmith Middle Fauresmith Lower Fauresmith	} Wet. (Intense erosion.)
. . . .	An arid period.
Upper Stellenbosch Middle Stellenbosch Lower Stellenbosch	} Wet? (Intense erosion.)
. . . .	?
Pebble Culture	Wet? (Intense erosion.)

In 1929, during a brief visit to the Transvaal, I myself found a number of pebble tools in some of the terrace gravels of the Vaal River, and similar finds have been recorded by Wayland, who visited South Africa, and by van Riet Lowe and other South African prehistorians. For a long time the geological age of these pebble tools was uncertain, and although *typologically* they were of an earlier phase than the great hand-axe culture, their earlier age could not be stated as a fact because we know from elsewhere that simple pebble tools persisted long after the hand-axe culture was fully developed, in much the same way that candles still survive in these days of electric lighting. Recently, however, Professor van Riet Lowe has been working in conjunction with geologists of the Geological Survey of the Union of South Africa, and one of the very important results of this work is to date the 'pebble' culture of South Africa as older than the hand-axe culture on geological evidence, thus confirming the typological evidence.

It would seem, from the information at my disposal, that at present there is no site where this pebble culture has been found in association with its contemporary fauna. At the same time there is indirect evidence (which we must hope will soon be either proved or disproved by new discoveries) that the fauna was definitely archaic and included a species of Mastodon as well as the more primitive elephants. The pebble tools have been found *in situ* at River View Estate and elsewhere in the 60-foot terrace of the Vaal River, and at other places a 60-foot terrace has yielded this archaic fauna. Caution is, however, needed because it does not at all *necessarily* follow that a terrace at 60 feet above present level in one part of the Vaal Valley is of the same age as a terrace at a similar altitude elsewhere.

At present no subdivision of the pebble culture in South Africa is attempted, but it is possible that this will be done later. In East Africa there is certainly a twofold division and, as we have seen, Mr. Wayland makes even more divisions than that.

In South Africa the great hand-axe culture is represented by a very vast amount of material, and at present the South African prehistorians divide this into three main divisions which they call Lower, Middle, and Upper Stellenbosch respectively. In his latest paper Goodwin, in summarizing the sequence of cultures in South Africa, gives a table from van Riet Lowe showing what he considers to be their European and North African parallels; and the part of the table referring to the Stellenbosch is as follows:

South African stage.	*European equivalent.*
Victoria West Industry	Acheulean+proto-Levallois+
Stellenbosch ⎧ Upper	Clacton+
⎨ Middle	Chellean+Clacton+
⎩ Lower	Old Chellean+

Professor H. Breuil, however, places the Middle Stellenbosch as the equivalent of the early Acheulean of Europe, and the Upper Stellenbosch as the equivalent of the later Acheulean. Breuil apparently regards the Victoria West variation of the Stellenbosch as a prelude to the Levalloisian or, as Goodwin and van Riet Lowe call it, a proto-Levalloisian.

From what I have seen myself and from the general measure of agreement among other authorities, there seems little doubt that the Lower Stellenbosch may be regarded as essentially the same as the Chellean part of the great hand-axe culture. It is, of course, a South African manifestation of that stage, but it seems to me a great pity that the term 'Stellenbosch' is still used to describe it instead of employing the word Chellean with the qualifying words 'South African' if thought necessary.

We have seen that in East Africa the discovery of large numbers of implements of the Chellean part of the hand-axe culture in well stratified deposits, as at Oldoway, has made it possible to establish a series of evolutionary stages of the Chellean. At present no such subdivision is possible in South Africa, but I feel sure that, now that the study of the Prehistory of South Africa has entered upon a phase in which great attention is being paid to stratigraphical geological evidence, some sort of division will sooner or later be necessary.

While I was in the Transvaal, Dr. Solomon and I found a site where the only implements present were pebble tools and the very crudest form of hand-axes—an assemblage which is the exact equivalent of the first stage of the Chellean in East Africa. These hand-axes were much more primitive than many which in the museums were described as Lower Stellenbosch, many of which were more comparable to much later stages of the Chellean.

I, personally, have seen so very little of the material which is described as Middle Stellenbosch that I cannot give a first-hand opinion. From illustrations, however, and from what has been said in descriptions, it seems to me likely that the term Middle Stellenbosch includes both the final (or transitional) stage of the East African Chellean as well as the earlier Acheulean stages. The presence of cleavers in common association with the Middle Stellenbosch hand-axes at some sites very strongly suggests that part, at least, of the Middle Stellenbosch is the equivalent of the earlier stages of the East African Acheulean.

G

We turn next to the Upper Stellenbosch. At two sites, assemblages classified as Upper Stellenbosch have been found *in situ* under what we may call ideal conditions; that is to say, in definite association with a fossil fauna and in a position which shows clearly their stratigraphical relationship to the next South African culture stage which is called the Fauresmith culture. Both these discoveries are due to Professor van Riet Lowe, both are situated in the valley of the Vaal River, but they are about ninety miles apart. The first site is Sheppard Island,[1] where the 'D' gravels yielded 'thousands of coups de poing and biseaux' which are regarded as 'belonging to the Upper Stellenbosch'. The 'vast majority of the implements are worked on large flakes'; but, on the other hand, there is no reference whatever to the presence of what is known as the 'Victoria West' type of core. Professor van Riet Lowe informs me that he thinks that in spite of this the implements at the Sheppard Island site were made on flakes which were obtained by a 'Victoria West core' technique, but I am not wholly satisfied on this point.

The evidence at Sheppard Island shows quite clearly that the makers of the assemblages found in these 'D' gravels had been living at the site before the formation of this gravel bed had started, and that they continued to live there throughout the period in which those gravels were being deposited. In other words, the assemblage represents a considerable period of time.

The other site is on the River View Estates, opposite Windsorton.[2] Here, in the gravels of the lowermost

---

[1] 'Further Notes on the Archaeology of Sheppard Island', C. van Riet Lowe in *S.A. Journal of Science*, vol. xxvi, pp. 165 et seqq.

[2] 'Implementiferous Gravels of the Vaal River at River View Estate', *Nature*, vol. 136, p. 53, July 1935.

terrace, there has been found a great abundance of rolled and unrolled Upper Stellenbosch tools, and the completely mineralized remains of a variety of extinct animals. Professor van Riet Lowe further tells us that

'In this Upper Stellenbosch congeries we have further definite proof, were this indeed required, that the so-called Victoria West industry merely represents the factory site débris of the Upper Stellenbosch Culture, for in addition to very many fine hand axes and cleavers worked on flakes we found numbers of detaching hammers and typical Victoria West cores from which the flakes used for these axes and cleavers were struck.'

It had in the past been argued by many South African prehistorians, including van Riet Lowe himself, that the so-called Victoria West industry was in reality simply the factory débris of the Upper Stellenbosch, and the view had been expressed that it was a technique essentially due to certain forms of local material. Let me quote again from Lowe's Sheppard Island paper. After expressing the view that both the Fauresmith culture and the Victoria West industry are both merely localized variations with restricted geographical distribution, he continues:

'It is otherwise difficult to explain why both the Stellenbosch and Middle Stone Age industries extend over the length and breadth of Southern Africa while not only the Fauresmith but also the Victoria West appear, but for very occasional and often doubtful outliers, confined to very definite geological zones, the former to the Lydianite Zone of the Vaal Valley, and the latter to the Dolerite Zone of the Great Karoo.'

That was written in 1929; now in 1935 comes the discovery of this typical Upper Stellenbosch site at River View Estates, where the flakes for the hand-axes and cleavers were made by the Victoria West technique. At

River View Estates, however, instead of Dolerite 'the materials preferred comprise varieties of Ventersdorp lava and quartzites, the weathering properties of which are entirely different from those of Victoria West (Karoo) dolerites where insolation is common. No doubt whatever can be cast upon the purposeful shaping of these cores as a preliminary to the removal of the flakes that were ultimately trimmed into hand-axes and cleavers'.

This new discovery thus for all time disposes of the view that it was the particular material (dolerite) of the Victoria West area which was responsible for the Victoria West technique for obtaining large flakes from which hand-axes could be made.

On the other hand, the absence of this type of core from many sites, including the sites at Sheppard Island and Pniel (near Kimberley and not the Pniel in the Drachenstein Mts.) suggests to me that the Victoria West technique was not the only one used for obtaining flakes by the makers of the Upper Stellenbosch stage of culture. Only four miles from Pniel (near Kimberley) is the site of Barkly where the Victoria West technique was extensively used, and from a study of big collections from both sites, I suggest that it is by no means impossible that the 'typical Upper Stellenbosch' of Pniel and Sheppard Island, &c., is not the same as and must not be confused with, the equally 'typical Upper Stellenbosch' of such sites as River View Estates (Windsorton) and Vereeniging, &c. Although I can produce no definite evidence to support my view, I am inclined to believe that future work will reveal that these two divisions of the Upper Stellenbosch are not contemporary, but that one is earlier than the other.[1]

[1] Professor van Reit Lowe, to whom this chapter was sent in typescript, dissents from the view and holds that all the Upper

There is another important problem in connexion with the Upper Stellenbosch of South Africa. Where the 'Victoria West' technique was employed to obtain the flakes which were made into hand-axes and cleavers, there was definitely a resemblance to the Levalloisian technique. That is to say, a core was very carefully prepared before the required flake was detached, and the flake shows a prepared or facetted striking platform. The question is whether this was a case of parallel evolution or whether the two techniques are more closely related. L'Abbé Breuil, as we have seen, considers that it is not impossible that the Victoria West technique may be the origin of the Levalloisian. I find this view hard to accept, for the early Levalloisian of Europe is contemporary with a stage of the Acheulean that is definitely less developed and probably older than the Upper Stellenbosch. There are two other alternative explanations.

If I am right in regarding the Upper Stellenbosch of such sites as Sheppard Island and Pniel as not due to a Victoria West technique, then it may be that contact between an early Levalloisian and the developed Stellenbosch of such sites as these led to a branch of the latter people adopting a suitably modified form of the Levalloisian technique for obtaining the large flakes that they required.

Or secondly, as it is decidedly noticeable that among the forms of the unstruck Victoria West cores there are many that have more than a resemblance to large, clumsy Chellean-type hand-axes, the possibility cannot yet be ruled out that the evolution of the Victoria West technique was a direct local development from an earlier and cruder stage of the Stellenbosch culture without any Levalloisian

Stellenbosch culture material is associated with the Victoria West technique.

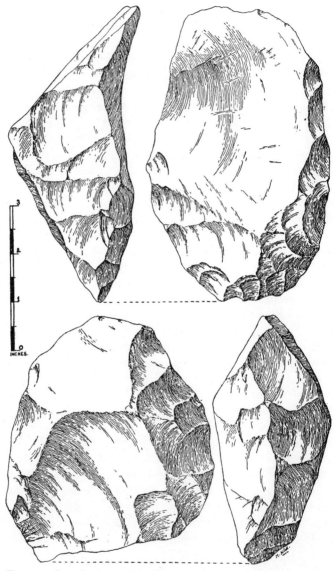

FIG. 10. Struck cores of the Victoria West type, Upper Stellenbosch culture (from Barkly, S. Africa)

influence. I can conceive of it being quite possible that a craftsman, in finishing off a large Chellean hand-axe, may have struck a false blow which removed a large piece

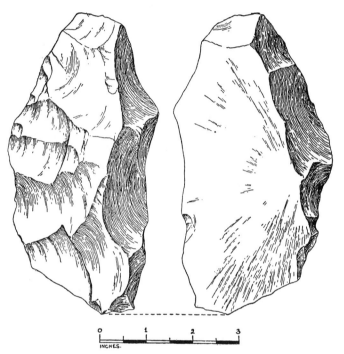

FIG. 11. An untrimmed flake from a Victoria West core (from Barkly, S. Africa)

of his unfinished tool in the form of a big flake, that he then took this large flake and made from it a smaller and neater hand-axe, and from this developed the idea of the Victoria West technique. I do not say this did happen, but that I can easily conceive of its having happened.

Before leaving the Stellenbosch culture and passing on to the Fauresmith, I must comment upon the question of terminology. In his note in *Nature* on the River View Estate site, van Riet Lowe writes, in discussing the Victoria West technique in relation to the Upper Stellenbosch culture: 'Once this special technique is understood, and it is realized what a great proportion of the tools are cleavers the necessity for breaking away from the use of such terms as Chellean and Acheulean will be more readily appreciated.'

I very strongly contest this view. I grant that the Upper Stellenbosch of South Africa has a far higher proportion of cleavers than the Acheulean stages of the hand-axe culture in Europe. I grant, too, that the technique of the Victoria West division of the Upper Stellenbosch is one not found in Europe, but I cannot see that this is justification for the continued use of the word Stellenbosch to describe the South African hand-axe cultures. So long as the leading South African prehistorians continue to use the term 'Stellenbosch' those of us who work in other areas must follow their lead, but I hope that in the interests of all prehistorians they will sooner or later adopt a more logical terminology.

I have made no attempt to indicate the distribution of the various stages of the Stellenbosch culture in South Africa because I am not in a position to do so. As we have already seen two sites in South Africa have now yielded good geological evidence that the culture group which is described as the Fauresmith culture follows the upper stages of the Stellenbosch culture. This has been established not only at Sheppard Island but also at River View Estate, Windsorton, where it is later than the Upper Stellenbosch, which is there associated with cores of the Victoria West type. Thus we may say definitely that even if it be subsequently shown that there are, as I think likely, two divisions of the Upper Stellenbosch with different techniques for obtaining the large flakes from which most of the tools were made, the Fauresmith culture is, nevertheless, proved to be younger than both of them.

One of the remarkable things about the recorded evidence is the limited distribution of the Fauresmith culture, which seems to be confined to an area where lydianite occurs. This is at present attributed by South African prehistorians to the fact that Lydianite alone provided a suitable material for this culture. I find this view exceedingly hard to accept because, in my own experience in East Africa, I have found that material has very little effect upon cultures. The hand-axes of Acheulean stage found at Oldoway are very largely made from a most intractable quartzite, and yet in beauty and skill of execution they compare very closely with hand-axes of the Fauresmith culture. Similarly, flakes and blades resembling those of the Fauresmith culture can be made in many other materials, so that I feel that if the distribution of the Fauresmith culture does prove on further investigation to be limited to one small area, another explanation must be sought and the material must not be used as an argument.[1] The Union of South Africa is a very large area, and I personally believe that sooner or later the Fauresmith culture will be found to have a much wider distribution.[2]

Turning to the characteristics of the culture itself we find that, while small and extremely well-made hand-axes are the commonest implements, they are associated with long points and blades, and also with side scrapers.

[1] In his latest paper van Riet Lowe shows that Fauresmith implements of quartzite and lava are now being found.

[2] In a typescript note to me early in 1936 Lowe writes: 'We find Upper Fauresmith tools over many thousands of square miles.'

These are usually made from flakes struck from cores that have been prepared by a Levalloisian technique, and the bulb-ends of the flakes have well-made facetted striking platforms. In other words, the Fauresmith culture has characteristics of two distinct culture groups, the great Chelleo-Acheulean hand-axe culture and the great Levalloisian one.

Such a state of affairs is not in the least unusual. As I have shown in my book, *Adam's Ancestors*, the result of the contact of these two culture groups in Europe, Palestine, and in Africa has always been that some sort of culture fusion has occurred. In Europe, cultures such as those named after La Micoque and Combe Capelle are excellent examples of this. In Palestine, Dr. Dorothy Garrod has shown us that a similar fused culture occurs. In East Africa the Nanyukian gives another example; and so on. (The fusion of culture does not necessarily imply a fusion of the races or species which were originally responsible for the distinct cultures, and, in fact, where two cultures came into contact the races responsible for them may each borrow certain ideas from the other so that two or more modified cultures, each reflecting the effect of contact, may develop. Present-day Africa has many examples of this for us.

At first view, then, the Fauresmith culture represents a fusion between a Levalloisian and an Upper Stellenbosch (or late Acheulean) stage of culture. But I am not sure that this 'first view' is correct. In discussing the Upper Stellenbosch it was pointed out that the division which has the Victoria West type of core has very marked resemblances in technique to the Levalloisian, so much so that Professor Breuil remarked that it might almost be regarded as proto-Levalloisian—a view long held by Professor van Riet Lowe.

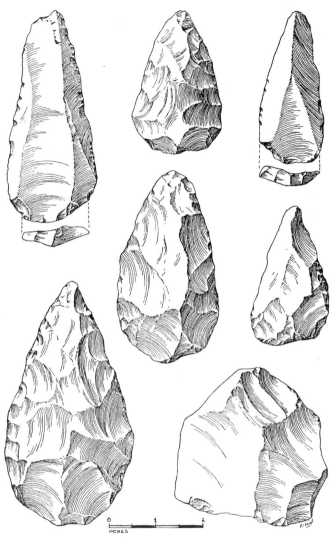

INCHES

FIG. 12. Hand-axes, flakes, and a core of the Fauresmith culture from Fauresmith, Orange Free State (compare with Fig. 5)

Bearing that in mind, and bearing the possibility of parallel evolution also in mind, I think it *more than possible* that the Fauresmith culture represents a direct evolution from that division of the Stellenbosch which has the Victoria West type of core. And here I must mention that, although in that earlier stage the cores have *in the majority of cases* a form recalling the clumsy hand-axe, there are also cores in the Victoria West assemblages which are of a more normal Levalloisian shape, as, for example, its so-called 'horse-shoe' cores.

The Fauresmith culture is at present divided into three major divisions, Lower, Middle, and Upper, and in this the South African prehistorians have the support of Professor Breuil who, however, adds a word of warning that much further study is required. I must confess that I do not know the details of the typological differences in these three divisions, save that it appears that the implements become smaller and finer and the Levalloisian type cores and flakes more evolved. We must hope that before long the Bureau of Archaeology will publish details of the divisions with full illustrations, for in this respect the by now out-of-date volume published by Goodwin and van Riet Lowe, called *The Stone Age Cultures of South Africa*, gives us very little guidance.

Before we pass on to the next group of cultures in South Africa I must remind my readers that the available South African evidence suggests that the period during which the Fauresmith culture flourished is apparently separated from the earlier period of the Stellenbosch culture by an arid or semi-arid period. This may account for the apparent lack of absolute links between the Upper Stellenbosch (of the Victoria West division) and the Lower Fauresmith; links which I suggest will one day be found in some other part of the Union.

Similarly, there is evidence that at the end of the time of the Fauresmith culture an arid period set in. So far as the faunal evidence goes, and it is not far at present, it seems as though the arid period between the time of the Stellenbosch culture and the time of the Fauresmith one was sufficiently intense to cause the extinction of many species which are associated with the former culture.

With the Fauresmith culture only a few extinct animals, such as *Equus capensis* and *Bubalus bainii* occur, while there are many species similar to those of the present day.

Following the arid period, which marks the close of the time when the Upper stage of the Fauresmith flourished, the climate became again more humid, and during this next period the Stone Age cultures are represented by what is commonly described as the Middle Stone Age complex of South Africa.

In the summary of the present position edited by Goodwin and published at the end of 1935, only four different groups or divisions of the Middle Stone Age complex are given, but many South African prehistorians would agree that there are many more. The real difficulty is that at present, although tool assemblages belonging to this period are very common, there is very little evidence of their stratigraphical relationship to each other. It seems highly probable that in point of fact a number of distinct human groups were scattered over South Africa, each with a variation or modification of a developed Levalloisian culture. If this is true it means that the relative chronological sequence cannot be worked out until a great many sites with a good stratigraphy have been worked; for when different divisions of a single major culture are contemporaneous and, what is more, are each evolving contemporaneously over a fairly long period, one site may give one sequence, say A B C, while a second may give B A C, and a third C B A.

The four divisions listed in Goodwin's summary in 1935 are Glen Grey, Howieson's-Poort, Pietersberg, and Stillbay. Of these the first compares very closely with the Upper Levalloisian of East Africa, and, so far as I can judge from the evidence available to me, it represents a more or less pure developed Levalloisian type of culture. With the Pietersberg division I am not personally acquainted, nor can I find, in the books and papers which I have, any illustrations of it, so I can say nothing about it. The other two divisions, Stillbay and Howieson's-Poort, to which we may add also the Mossel-bay variation, are undoubtedly the result of a contact or fusion between people making a developed Levalloisian stage of culture and some off-shoot of the late Aurignacian such as that called Upper Kenya Aurignacian phase C.

I can find no record of any site in the Union of South Africa at which a pure Aurignacian type of culture occurs,[1] and at the moment it would seem as though—in the case of those divisions which show a fusion—the contact occurred farther north. As we shall see in another chapter, there is evidence from Southern Rhodesia to support this.

Until a very great deal more detailed study of the so-called Middle Stone Age of South Africa has been carried out, little more can be said than I have said above. The industry found at Stillbay in which fine leaf-shaped points, beautifully retouched all over both surfaces, are the type tools, seems to me to represent a true culture

---

[1] Mazeppa Bay and the area round it has, however, yielded assemblages in which Aurignacian types predominate over Levalloisian. See a paper entitled 'Giant Crescents' by van Riet Lowe in *Transactions of the Royal Society of South Africa*, 1931, vol. xix.

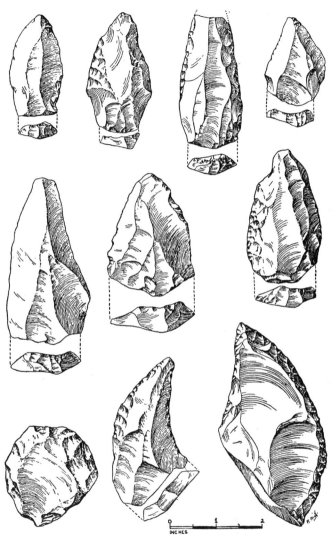

INCHES

FIG. 13. A Middle Stone Age assemblage from Basutoland
(Millard Collection)

which is very widespread, and possibly we shall eventually have to regard assemblages such as those from Howieson's-Poort as simply divisions of a Stillbay culture as distinct from an Upper Levalloisian one.

Before passing on to the next South African division of the Stone Age, I must issue a warning to my readers in connexion with the name 'Middle Stone Age' complex. In *time* this group belongs not to the Middle Pleistocene *but* to the very end of the Upper Pleistocene, immediately preceding the Holocene or Recent period. The word 'Middle' does not even imply that the Middle Stone Age complex occurs in date between the Lower Palaeolithic and the Upper Palaeolithic, for in point of fact it takes the place of the latter in South Africa. For this reason it is to be hoped that the South African prehistorians will devise a new term to describe this culture complex as soon as possible.

The Middle Stone Age complex was apparently followed in South Africa by two distinct cultures, each of which is capable of a certain amount of division stratigraphically and typologically as well as regionally. These two cultures are termed the Smithfield culture and the Wilton culture.

In the former the most common tool is the end scraper, while crescents and 'backed blades' to all intents and purposes do not occur. In the Wilton culture the most typical tools are, on the other hand, crescents and other small geometric microliths, together with small double-end and thumb-nail scrapers.

One branch of the Wilton culture is essentially associated with shell-mounds, as is also the case in East Africa, and this shell-mound or Kitchen Midden division, as well as the later stages of the true Wilton and true Smithfield cultures, seem to have continued until only a hundred or so years ago, for in some sites copper trade wire and trade beads occur.

The position of the culture sequence in South Africa as I see it may thus be tabulated as follows:

HOLOCENE OR RECENT	Wilton { Upper, Middle, Lower Smithfield { Upper, Middle, Lower	(Two culture groups evolving contemporaneously in post-Pleistocene times down to a very short time ago. The 'Neolithic' elements of South Africa are probably later than the dawn of these cultures but earlier than the later developments.) Also shell-mound variants.
UPPER PLEISTOCENE	'Middle Stone Age' Complex { Stillbay, Howieson's-Poort, Pietersburg, Gley Grey, Mossel-bay, Mazeppa, &c.	(The relative chronological sequence of these and many other variants as yet not clear. Some were contemporary with each other. Gley Grey *may be* earliest.)
	HIATUS IN THE SEQUENCE	
	Fauresmith { Upper, Middle, Lower ↑	(Although there is no direct evidence it is highly possible that a pure early Levalloisian was also present at this time.)
	HIATUS IN THE SEQUENCE	
MIDDLE PLEISTOCENE	Upper Stellenbosch Variant B with Victoria West cores Upper Stellenbosch Variant A without Victoria West cores	(These two may be contemporary divisions of the Upper Stellenbosch evolving side by side from the Middle Stellenbosch, or possibly variant B is slightly later than A and denotes an Upper Stellenbosch which is being affected by Levalloisian influences.)
	Middle Stellenbosch ↑	(Will probably require a good deal of subdivision: includes assemblages which appear to be late Chellean in form and others which distinctly show Acheulean technique in flaking.)
	Lower Stellenbosch	(Mainly Chellean forms, associated in some cases with flakes recalling Clactonian which *may represent the presence, as yet unproved, of a distinct and separate early flake culture*.)
LOWER PLEISTOCENE	Pre-Chellean pebble tools	

Finally, mention must be made of the discovery in South Africa from time to time of polished axes and of barbed arrowheads, which are grouped together as 'Neolithic elements'. I am not aware of any find of this having yet been made under conditions which show the relationship of this Neolithic element to the Wilton or Smithfield cultures, but in his table Goodwin put it last of all, presumably on typological grounds. Both the axes and the barbed arrows suggest affinities with the Tumbian culture of the Congo, and probably represent infiltrations of influences from that area, if not actual migrations of people.

CHAPTER VI

THE STONE AGE CULTURES OF
NORTH AFRICA

FOR the purposes of this book I am going to divide the
North African area into two regions and deal with each
separately. First of all we will examine what is known
about the Stone Age in the western part of the North
African coast, and with this area we will include the
Sahara. Then we will take Egypt and the northern part of
the Nile Valley.

The first of these two regions is mainly French territory,
and as might be expected in view of the fact that France
has so long led the world in Stone Age research, records
of the discovery of stone implements in this area are very
numerous and start about fifty years ago.

At the same time it is somewhat surprising that there
is not much more exact stratigraphical information than
there actually is. This is chiefly due to the fact that only
in comparatively recent years has the full value of stratigraphical evidence been appreciated. As a result we find
that, although there are extensive collections of stone implements belonging to the earlier part of the Pleistocene,
there is, in most cases, very little positive evidence of their
age, and typology alone has to be relied upon. The position
in regard to the cultures of the last part of the Pleistocene
is, however, much more satisfactory, and there are several
very important papers which deal with the cultures of this
period.

Before we turn to these we must, however, briefly see
what is known about the earlier cultures. Unfortunately,
much of what has been published about the Stone Age in
French North Africa is in publications which very seldom

are seen in England, so that the position of the English prehistorian who wants to know about them is made still more difficult. In 1931, in his paper on the 'Stone Age in Africa' published in *Cahiers d'Art*, Professor Breuil collected together and summarized a great deal of the information concerning this region, and those who want more data than I shall give are advised to refer to this article.

We have already seen in Chapter II, in our discussion of the fauna of the Stone Age, that during the earliest part of the Pleistocene period (sometimes considered as Pliocene) North African fauna was of a more archaic type than that which has been found in association with stone tools belonging to the great hand-axe culture. Unfortunately, however, there seems to be as yet no positive evidence of the presence of any pre-Chellean stage of culture in the earlier deposits, and the first recognized Stone Age culture of the region is the great hand-axe culture, the Chelleo-Acheulean.

Assemblages of implements belonging indubitably to the great hand-axe culture have been found at many widely separated points in the region we are considering, and from the typological point of view it seems fairly clear that a number of stages of evolution are represented. Thus the quartzite implements from Clairefontaine collected from gravel deposits by Messrs. Latapie and Reygasse are typologically early Chellean, although the same region has also yielded typically Acheulean hand-axes.

Immense collections of stone implements have been found in the depression of Lake Karar, and some of these were collected by Gentil in direct association with the remains of fossil animals which were studied by Professor Boule. The stone tools of this collection belong typologically to a developed stage of the Chellean and to the

Acheulean, and the fauna is comparable with that found at Oldoway with similar stages of the hand-axe culture.

Associated with a very similar fauna was a collection of implements from Ternifine which, however, were of Chellean type only. In a good many instances implements of Chellean and Acheulean type have been found in consolidated gravels and sand, of obviously great age but without direct evidence of their relationship to other stages of culture, while in the Sahara region finds of hand-axes on old land surfaces beneath the sand have been frequently made, but with no evidence of age other than that of typology. It may be definitely stated, however, that wherever an associated fauna has been found with the Chelleo-Acheulean culture in North Africa, the fauna shows clearly that this great culture is older than the so-called Mousterian (or Aterian) of the same region.

One of the most valuable papers on the age of the later stages of the Acheulean is that by Professor R. Vaufray, published in 1932 in the *Revue de Géographie Physique*[1], under the heading of 'Les Plissements Acheulo-Mousteriens des Alluvions de Gafsa'. This paper followed a special visit to investigate a site first recorded by Dr. Colignon in 1886 and subsequently discussed by many other writers. Vaufrey finds that the ancient deposits, which contain a developed stage of the Acheulean in their higher horizons, have been seriously affected by a folding movement which, however, has not disturbed deposits which contain a 'Mousterian' stage of culture. Thus he has been able to demonstrate that during an interval between the periods when the Acheulean and the Mousterian, respectively, flourished, there were marked disturbances of the earth's crust. This fact is of particular interest to us because of its similarity with the

[1] Vol. v, Paris, 1932.

evidence from East Africa where, at the close of the time of the Acheulean stage of culture, very violent faulting occurred.

One of the best-known and most often quoted sites of the hand-axe culture in French North Africa is the ancient lake basin of Tabelbalat. All round this ancient basin are sites which have yielded vast quantities of stone implements of very many stages of culture, showing that in Pleistocene times, when there was a lake there, this region was thickly inhabited.

The Tabelbalat site, known as Tachenghit, has in particular yielded very beautiful material belonging to the hand-axe culture, and some writers have spoken of it as the Tachenghit culture. From the material which I have seen and from that figured in various publications, the greater part of the Tachenghit material seems to compare very closely indeed with Acheulean stages 3 and 4 of the East African sequence.

One cannot help feeling that in some of these old lake basins there must be places where excavation would reveal a sequence of the evolutionary stages of the hand-axe culture, which would be far more satisfactory than any quantity of material divided up upon a purely typological basis, which is all that is possible at present. Writing about the Tabelbalat region Professor Breuil remarks:

'The types are not uniform from one site to another; and there is certainly a need to distinguish several facies of different ages. Some of the more primitive specimens are also more deeply patinated: one can suspect a Chellean stage, followed by ovates which are far better worked and also less patinated, then finely made lance-shaped hand axes associated with many cleavers, which are far less common in Algeria. . . .'

It may be pointed out here that the cleavers found with the developed Acheulean in North Africa are very similar indeed to those from East and South Africa which accompany similarly developed stages of the Acheulean.

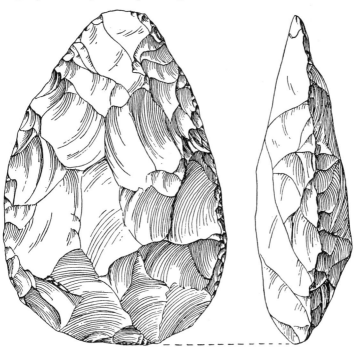

FIG. 14. Hand-axe of late Acheulean type from Sbaïka, Algeria
(¾ actual size)

NOTE: The term Sbaïkan was apparently first used to denote the late stage of the hand-axe culture, but it has since been applied to many other types of implement, including the leaf-shaped tools which are associated with the Aterian. The term is therefore no longer of much value and should be abandoned.

While the hand-axe culture is by far the commonest and best-known of the earlier Stone Age cultures in North Africa, it is necessary to point out that Professor Breuil and others record the presence of sites where assemblages recalling the Clactonian of Europe occur. Much more work is, however, required before it can be stated categorically that a Clactonian culture occurs in North Africa.

Following the great hand-axe culture in North Africa comes a culture which in most of the literature dealing with North Africa is described as Mousterian.

There are a very great many sites which have yielded this flake culture and a number of distinct stages are recognizable. Both faunistic and geological evidence, where available, shows that it is later in time than the close of the period which was marked by the presence of the great hand-axe culture.

Professor Breuil and others regard the early stages of this so-called 'Mousterian' as a typical developed Levalloisian which in turn is replaced by a more normal Mousterian. The Mousterian proper is replaced by a local derivative in which tanged points are characteristic. This Mousterian with tanged points is known as Aterian, and some writers claim that it has several distinct stages—a claim which seems to be well founded.

According to Professor Breuil there is a site called Sidi Mansour,[1] not far from Gafsa, which was discovered by M. Boudy. Here there is a section some 15 metres in thickness which has yielded the following stratigraphical evidence.

At the base there is a horizon which yields a developed Levalloisian (or early Mousterian, as the finder called it). Next, there is a level with typical Mousterian forms, but no trace of the tanged points which characterize the Aterian. Higher up is a deposit with much typical Aterian

---

[1] Professor Vaufrey, in a letter to me, states that he entirely disagrees with the interpretation of the evidence at Sidi Mansour.

material, while implements belonging to the Capsian occur at the top.

Somewhat similar sequences have been found elsewhere in North Africa, and there seems to be little doubt that the three lower horizons represent the normal sequence of evolution of the Levalloisian-Aterian culture.

The Aterian culture is of particular interest for a number of reasons. It undoubtedly represents a local development from the Levalloisian-Mousterian complex. One of its typical artefacts is the so-called 'tanged Mousterian' point which is of itself interesting because it is a more or less unique development in a culture stage of this period (it extends, however, to the other North African region, the Nile Valley). Another typical implement of the Aterian, particularly in its later stages of development, is the leaf-shaped point trimmed delicately all over both surfaces and strongly recalling both the Solutrean leaf-shaped tools of Europe, and the Stillbay culture of East and South Africa.

At very many sites in French North Africa there is clear evidence that the cultures known as Capsian and Ibero-Maurusian are of later date than the Mousterian and the early Aterian, but it is possible that the *later stages* of the Aterian may have been contemporaneous with these cultures in some districts, especially in the fringes of the Sahara. In addition to this it must be noted that, on typological grounds, it seems highly probable that some of the North African Neolithic divisions were derived from a final development of the Aterian, so that we have indirect evidence suggesting that the Aterian had, in some areas, a continuous and slow evolution from the time that it first appeared right on up to the end of the Stone Age.

Turning from the Aterian proper we find that in most

areas it was followed by one or other of the two cultures which, though very similar in many respects, have certain features which separate them markedly. These two cultures are the Capsian and the culture which was known until recently as the Ibero-Maurusian. The latter culture was so named because it was thought that it was represented both in North Africa and in the Iberian peninsula, but in a recent paper Vaufrey and Gobert have shown that this is not the case and, as the name is thus misleading, they suggest that in future the Ibero-Maurusian should be called Oranian. With this suggestion I entirely agree, and in the rest of this chapter I shall speak of it as Oranian but will put (I-M) after it, for the sake of clearness.

A good deal of very careful excavation has been carried out at both Capsian and Oranian (I-M) sites, and in consequence there is good evidence both of the associated fauna and also of the human types which represent the makers of this culture.

Let us take the Capsian culture first of all. This culture has been known from North Africa for a very long time, and it was formerly generally regarded as the possible source of origin of the Aurignacian culture of France. This view has, however, not been confirmed, although it seems highly probable that towards the very end of the Pleistocene there was a movement of makers of the Capsian culture across into south Europe, taking with them an advanced stage of this culture, which is very similar indeed to the late Aurignacian culture of the South of Spain and the South of France. The arrival of the Capsian element in Europe, however, was apparently considerably after the earlier European Aurignacian elements had become established.

The most important recent study of the Capsian culture in North Africa is probably that of Professor R. Vaufrey, who in a paper in *L'Anthropologie* in 1933 under the title of 'Notes sur le Capsien' summarizes the results of test excavations carried out at some of the type sites.

He points out that the formerly held view, that micro-lithic tools are absent or very rare in the Lower Capsian, is entirely unfounded. Excavating at one of the type stations of the Lower Capsian, El Mekta, 15 kilometres north of Gafsa, he employed a very fine meshed riddle, with the result that he recovered numerous lunates and other microliths, in direct association with the implements usually regarded as more typical of the Lower Capsian, namely, large backed blades, burins, and end-scrapers. In other words Professor Vaufrey finds that the Lower Capsian implements of North Africa include many types which are not present in the earlier stages of the Aurignacian of Europe, and the assemblage which he describes compares very closely indeed with that which in East Africa I have called Upper Kenya Aurignacian phase b.

The Lower Capsian is followed, according to Vaufrey's latest investigations, by two distinct derivatives; that is to say, that there are two different Upper Capsian divisions. One of these he calls by the rather cumbersome name of Inter-capso-neolithic (formerly called Inter-getulo-neo-lithic) and the other he terms Upper Capsian. In the Inter-capso-neolithic large backed blades are very rare, and ordinary burins noted by their absence. On the other hand, the microlithic group of tools becomes more and more dominant, and micro-burins are very common. Perforated digging stones and saddle querns occur, and the whole assemblage may be regarded as, generally speaking, comparable to the Tardenoisian of Europe or the Wilton of Kenya.

The other derivative of the Lower Capsian is an Upper Capsian in which large backed blades become very rare, but in which burins still occur and the microlithic element becomes very much more geometric in form.

The final stage of evolution of the Capsian is in Neolithic times, when there is what Vaufrey terms the 'Néolithique de tradition capsienne'. This will be discussed presently.

In summarizing the position of the Capsian Vaufrey says:

'In spite of this clear evolution, the Capsian industries do not any the less form a homogeneous unit of which the cement is formed by microlithic elements, which are numerous and of a highly evolved type from the early Capsian where triangles, trazepes, and microburins are mixed with the more typical elements. From the point of view of typology the Capsian appears to us as an industry of Mesolithic character or, at most, a final stage of the Palaeolithic, and one cannot dream of describing it as ancestral to the Aurignacian. The geological evidence is not any more favourable to the antiquity of the Capsian.'

With this view I am entirely in agreement, since the Lower Capsian compares typologically, *not* with the earlier stages of the Aurignacian of East Africa, i.e. the Basal Aurignacian or the succeeding Lower Aurignacian, but rather with the evolved Upper Aurignacian of phases b and c, which belong to very much the end of the Pleistocene.

Before passing from the Capsian to the Oranian (formerly Ibero-Maurusian) mention must be made of the careful excavation of a Capsian site which was described in 1928 in a Bulletin of the Logan Museum (U.S.A.). The excavations were carried out at the shell-mound of Metcha-el-Arbi, and are important because of the careful study of the associated fauna and of the human remains found *in situ*. This report on Metcha-el-Arbi entirely supports Professor Vaufrey in that it shows that the Lower Capsian is associated with many microlithic elements.

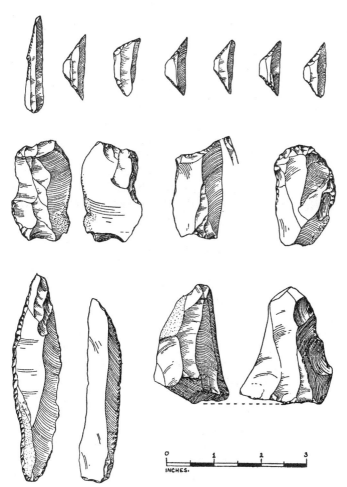

FIG. 15. Implements of the Lower Capsian culture of North
Africa (British Museum Collection)

Now we must turn to the Oranian (Ibero-Maurusian). Again we are indebted to Professor Vaufrey, this time in conjunction with Dr. Gobert, for an excellent, reasoned summary of the position of this culture, which was published in *L'Anthropologie* in 1932 under the title of 'Deux gisements extrêmes d'Ibéromaurusian'.

The Oranian (I-M) culture has a number of characters which link it with the Upper Capsian. Among these may be mentioned the presence of microliths, small backed blades and scrapers, and micro-burins. On the other hand, certain tool-types which are absolutely characteristic of the Capsian, such as large backed blades and angle burins, are missing from the Oranian except for a few very rare examples which are not at all typical.

From a study of the distribution of the Oranian (I-M) and the Upper Capsian, Vaufrey and others have come to the conclusion that they represent regional specializations, and the fact that the skulls found with each culture represent the same racial type supports this view.

Vaufrey finds that the Oranian shows very distinct evidence (in its earlier stages especially) that there are links between the Oranian (I-M) and some branch of the Aterian, for the cores of the Oranian culture show a persistence of the Levalloisian-Aterian technique.

The Oranian (I-M) culture seems to have been the absolute contemporary of the Upper Capsian, while it seems possible that in the region occupied by the makers of the Oranian culture the late stages of the Aterian may have been contemporary with the Lower Capsian elsewhere. The Oranian must, in fact, be regarded as representing a culture stage equivalent to the very final stage of the Upper Palaeolithic, continuing well on into the period commonly termed Mesolithic.

In discussing the Capsian culture, the excavations of

Metcha-el-Arbi by the Logan Museum were cited as giving
a picture of the culture with its associated fauna and
human types. For the Oranian (I-M) culture the recent
publication[1] on the excavation of two sites at Beni
Segoual serves the same purpose, and gives an excellent
picture of the culture, together with an account of its
associated fauna and human remains, and this publication
should be consulted by any who want a detailed account
of the Oranian (I-M) culture.

As we have seen, the final stages of the Capsian proper
were followed by a 'Neolithic of Capsian tradition'. We
have also seen that there is some evidence that in certain
regions the later stages of the Aterian, with their leaf-
shaped points and tanged blades, may have persisted and
developed, and finally given rise to some of the other
elements of the North African Neolithic.

Whatever may have been the diverse origins of the
different Neolithic elements in this area, it is safe to say
that there were several more or less distinct divisions of
the Neolithic, all of which are, however, characterized by
having arrow-heads and polished axes in greater or less
quantity, as well as much pottery.

In his paper in *Cahiers d'Art* Professor Breuil has given
many illustrations of the types of arrowhead found in the
North African Neolithic, and a very great variety of forms
is revealed.

Some are of particular interest because they give us
links with the arrowheads which go with the Tumbian
culture of the Congo, others link us with some of the
Neolithic cultures of the Nile Valley. Perhaps the most
interesting of all the Neolithic discoveries of French
North Africa comes from French North-West Africa at

[1] 'Les Grottes Paléolithiques des Beni-Segoual' in *Archives de
l'Institut de Paléontologie humaine*, Mémoire No. 13, Paris, Dec. 1934.

Taferjit and at Tamaya Mellet. From both these sites assemblages have been collected which have, in addition to polished axes, barbed arrowheads, and pottery, many fragments of bone harpoons, which recall in some ways those of the Upper Palaeolithic of Europe, but (to my mind) are still more like the long wooden and bone harpoons of some of the swamp-dwelling peoples on lakes such as Bangweolo in Northern Rhodesia. In this connexion it is worth noting that both these prehistoric settlements were near an old swamp. The finds were associated with remains of fish, mollusca, and hippopotamus.

In fact, by Neolithic times, the whole of North Africa (including much of what is now desert) from the Nile to the Atlantic seaboard seems to have been occupied by different tribes with a Neolithic culture which varied locally according to tribal use and to the effect of outside contacts. More than that I am not prepared to say, as all I could do would be to quote *in extenso* from Professor Breuil's paper.

The sequence of cultures in French North Africa, as far as at present known, can thus be summarized as follows.

The earliest recognized culture is the Chelleo-Acheulean hand-axe culture, with the possibility that a local Clactonian may be, in part, contemporary with it.

After the Acheulean, and separated from it by a period of earth movements, comes the Levalloisio-Mousterian which, from the evidence at a number of sites, can be shown to have developed gradually into the Lower Aterian or tanged Mousterian of the region. In time the Lower and Upper Aterian represent the Upper Palaeolithic period. Towards the close of the Pleistocene, the Aterian was followed by the Capsian in some regions and

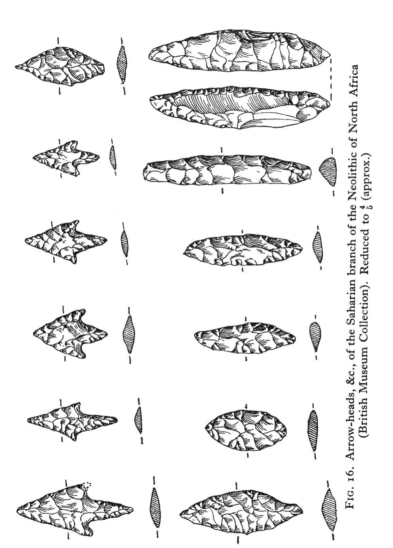

FIG. 16. Arrow-heads, &c., of the Saharian branch of the Neolithic of North Africa (British Museum Collection). Reduced to $\frac{4}{5}$ (approx.)

I

by the Oranian in others. Each of these had a series of evolutionary stages leading up to the Neolithic by way of a Mesolithic stage.

The Neolithic, which has many local divisions, is in part derived from the final stages of the Capsian, Oranian, and (in the Sahara region) a development of the Aterian, and in part is made up of elements coming from other areas.

Tabulated, the situation is as given below.

	Neolithic of Aterian origin	Neolithic of Oranian origin	Neolithic of Capsian origin
HOLOCENE		Developed Oranian Lower Oranian	Inter-capso-Neolithic Upper Capsian
UPPER PLEISTOCENE	Upper Aterian (*a*) Lower Aterian	Upper Aterian (*b*)	Lower Capsian
	Developed Levalloisian (or Mousterean) Early Levalloisian		
MIDDLE PLEISTOCENE	Acheulean Chellean	Clactonian?	
LOWER PLEISTOCENE	Pre-Chellean? (not yet recorded)		

We now pass on to the Nile Valley as representing the eastern part of the North African region. For information concerning this area we are chiefly dependent upon two sources; the work of Miss Caton Thompson and Miss Gardener in the Fayum depression and the Kharga Oasis, and the survey of the Nile Valley by Drs. Sandford and Arkell. In·addition to this comparatively recent work we have the study of the Kom-Ombo region, where M. Vignard discovered and elucidated the problems of the Sebilian culture.

It is a curious thing that, as in French North Africa, so in this other part of the North African region, there is as yet no definite and reliable record of any human culture which antedates the first appearance of the great Chelleo-

Acheulean hand-axe culture, and the question that arises is whether in both areas this is due to its absence or simply to the fact that investigators have not recognized it. In my own opinion the latter seems to be the more reasonable explanation, and I am convinced that in time pre-Chellean stages of culture will be found in North Africa in datable deposits.

Apart from the very important Acheulean discoveries made by Miss Caton Thompson at Kharga, which will be discussed presently, the great hand-axe culture in the Nile Valley has been more reliably studied by Drs. Sandford and Arkell than by anybody else. Their work, which is in course of being published in a series of volumes, is in the main a study of the Quaternary Geology of the Nile Valley, and as such is of considerable value. From the point of view of the prehistorian the earlier volumes of their study have been seriously marred by several features, some of which are still found in the latest publication. There is no definition given of what criteria have been used in deciding upon the division between Pliocene and Pleistocene, and, as mammalian fossil remains are almost entirely absent,[1] it is still more difficult for the reader to form his own opinion. Secondly, the volumes abound in such terms as 'the Chellean *Age*' (the italics are mine), while in the volume published in 1935 we still find essentially Levalloisian material described as Mousterian, which it most certainly is not.

[1] Recently, mammalian remains—which have not yet been published—have been found in the 100-ft. terrace; they are said to represent 'a markedly early Pleistocene fauna'. This statement does not necessarily mean that the fauna is earlier than that found with the hand-axe culture in other parts of Africa or in Europe, for all depends upon what definition of the word 'Pleistocene' is being referred to. Until details have been published judgement is reserved, but it seems likely that a Middle Pleistocene fauna is present.

The following table, derived from Dr. Sandford's 1935 publication *Palaeolithic Man, and the Nile Valley in Upper and Lower Egypt*, summarizes the position as he sees it.

150-ft. terrace.	No human implements found.
100-ft. terrace.	Primitive Chellean, Chellean and Chelleo-Acheulean, and early Acheulean, also the Egyptian form of the Clactonian.
50-ft. terrace.	Developed forms of the Acheulean with all the forms found in the 100-ft. terrace as derived material.
30-ft. terrace.	Early Mousterian flakes and cores, also Acheulean implements derived from the 50-ft. terrace. (Note: from the illustrations and description the 'Early Mousterian' specimens are in reality typically Levalloisian.)
⎰ 10- to 15-ft. terrace of Upper Egypt.	Typical Mousterian of Egypt. (This seems to be a later or developed Levalloisian [L.S.B.L.].)
⎱ 25-ft. gravels of Middle Egypt. Base of silts of Upper Egypt.	In part contemporary with the 10–15-ft. gravels and with the same types of tools, but also containing later forms.
Aggradation sites of Upper Egypt.	Final development of the Egyptian Mousterian (which has tanged points recalling the Aterian stage [L.S.B.L.] as well as Lower Sebilian.
Degradation gravels of Upper and Middle Egypt, suballuvial in the north.	Middle Sebilian.
Further degradation.	Upper Sebilian.
Accumulation.	End of Palaeolithic, then Neolithic to Recent. (Note: end of Mesolithic would be more accurate as the Middle and Upper Sebilian should be classed as Mesolithic [L.S.B.L.].)

From this table it is at once clear that a very great deal of work remains to be carried out (in connexion with the earlier cultures in particular) before the position can be regarded as satisfactory. The gravels of the 100-foot terrace contain implements of several stages of the Chellean part of the hand-axe culture, as well as both transitional Chelleo-Acheulean and early Chellean stages.

This in effect means that the earlier part of the evolution of the hand-axe culture in the Nile Valley occupies the time 'during the long interval between the abandoning of the 150-foot terrace and of the 100-foot level by the Nile'.

The later and more evolved stages of the Acheulean culture are not found in the 100-foot terrace gravels but do occur in the 50-foot terrace. There is no record of the earlier Levalloisian being also present in the 50-foot terrace, and in this, too, the position is similar to that in French North Africa where the Levalloisian comes *after* the final Acheulean.

This North African state of affairs is so unlike that of Europe or of East and South Africa as to be worthy of comment. It can only mean one of two things. Either in the North African region, with its comparatively few finds of *in situ* material of this period, the presence of a Levalloisian culture contemporary with the later stages of the Acheulean has been overlooked, or else the early Levalloisian of Europe and of East and South Africa respectively are derived from different sources and are not linked up across the North African region. Personally, I think that the first alternative gives the more likely explanation.

Before we leave the hand-axe culture and pass on to the Levalloisian, Mousterian, and Aterian cultures, we must refer to the exceptionally important find of an Acheulean site at Kharga. Here Miss Caton Thompson found a 'floor' from which over 500 Acheulean hand-axes were obtained. The floor was covered by the deposits laid down by a spring. As the full account of the work at Kharga has not yet been completed we have only preliminary reports to which to refer. The stage of culture represented by this Acheulean assemblage seems to be something comparable to the last stages of the Acheulean in East Africa, and evidence was obtained which showed that it was stratigraphically older than the Levalloisian and Aterian sites in the same region. Unfortunately, no associated mammalian fauna had been preserved. Following the hand-axe culture in the Nile Valley comes the Levalloisian which, as elsewhere in North Africa, develops into something closely resembling a true Mousterian. This Mousterian, or developed Levalloisian stage, is then followed by a local development (due probably to contact with Capsian influences). In one of the preliminary reports on Kharga, Miss Caton Thompson illustrates a series of implements belonging to this development of the Mousterian, and writes:

'I publish here a representative series of implements in Fig. 4 since they introduce a totally new factor into the subject of the Mousterian culture of Egypt. . . . Without opportunity for comparative study, I have provisionally called this industry Aterian on the strength of the tanged points. But as the neanthropic features of the French North African Aterian— namely, end scrapers, nosed scrapers, &c.—are absent in our industry, *whilst the laurel leaves introduce an element absent in the Aterian of Algeria and Tunisia*, I use the designation with reservations.' (The italics are mine.)

The absence of end-scrapers in association with the Aterian of Kharga may or may not be significant, but the presence of laurel leaf-shaped points trimmed all over both faces is entirely in keeping with the French North African Aterian,[1] as we have already seen, and I think it may be safely said that at most the Egyptian Aterian differs very little from that farther west.

[1] I understand that in a recent lecture Miss Caton Thompson supported this view and withdrew the statement which I have put in italics above.

If the Aterian is to be regarded as one local development of the Levalloisio-Mousterian of Egypt, the Sebilian, first found at the Kom-Ombo region and subsequently in many other places, must be similarly regarded as another. The cores and method of striking the primary flakes in the Lower Sebilian very strongly recall the Levalloisian technique, but the secondary trimming is strikingly reminiscent of that used by the Capsian peoples. It would, indeed, seem as though, as in the case of the Stillbay culture of South and East Africa, the Sebilian culture evolved locally from the results of a culture contact. At Kom-Ombo, M. Vignard has demonstrated the main stages of evolution of the Sebilian from its lower to its upper stages, in which microliths become dominant. Vignard and others have suggested that the Sebilian may be the ancestral form of all the microlithic cultures in Europe, North Africa, and elsewhere, but I see no reason for taking such a view.

At Kom-Ombo, Vignard was able to collect a mammalian fauna in association with the Sebilian culture, and this, although mainly consisting of species still living elsewhere in Africa, includes an extinct buffalo, and one or two other species which suggest a late Pleistocene age for the culture. The Lower Sebilian is, in fact, probably of an age comparable to the Lower Capsian and Oranian of North Africa and to the final stages of the Upper Aurignacian and of the Stillbay culture of East Africa. At one or two sites in the Nile Valley, assemblages of implements strongly recalling the Capsian have been found. One such rather incomplete series from Hilwan has been published by Dr. Sandford, while Miss Caton Thompson has also found such assemblages at Kharga. I am not aware of any direct stratigraphical evidence, however, which shows the relationship of this type of culture to the Sebilian or Aterian, with which it is probably contemporary. The final stages of the Sebilian in Egypt are probably to be regarded as Mesolithic, and it will be surprising if there is not also found one day a late and Mesolithic stage of the Aterian, tending in the direction of the Neolithic proper.

There are a number of divisions of the Egyptian Neolithic of which the best known are the Badarian, the Tasian, the Merimbdian, and the Neolithic of the Fayum. An excellent study of the latter has been written by Miss Caton Thompson and published in the monograph on the Fayum Depression.[1] The Fayum Neolithic has abundant evidences of agriculture in the form of sickle blades and querns, while actual basketwork granaries were also found. Polished axes occur, and diverse forms of arrowheads. The Badarian differs in a number of ways from the other Neolithic cultures, but it is not unlike the Neolithic from Tamaya Mellet.

The Nile Valley Stone Age cultures can be summarized in the following table:

HOLOCENE	Tasian, Merimbdian, Badarian, the Fayum Neolithic, &c.		
			Upper Sebilian Middle Sebilian
UPPER PLEISTOCENE	Capsian (? contemporary)	Aterian ↑ Egyptian Mousterian (or developed Levalloisian) Levalloisian	Lower Sebilian ↗
MIDDLE PLEISTOCENE	Late Acheulean Early Acheulean Transitional Chelleo-Acheulean Chellean }	Egyptian 'Clactonian'	
LOWER PLEISTOCENE	Pre-Chellean (not yet found for certain)		

[1] Special publication of the Royal Anthropological Institute.

CHAPTER VII

THE STONE AGE CULTURES OF WEST AND CENTRAL AFRICA (OTHER THAN EAST AFRICA)

UNDER this heading I shall group together a number of African territories where discoveries of Stone Age material have been recorded, but where there is as yet very little detailed evidence of the culture sequence. Of the countries to be discussed Southern Rhodesia alone has yielded important stratigraphical evidence of the culture sequence, but even there the story is much less complete than in East or even South Africa.

Much of what we know of the Stone Age in Southern Rhodesia we owe to the untiring work of the Rev. Neville Jones, while the valuable excavation of Bambata Cave by Mr. A. L. Armstrong yielded very important results indeed. Other keen students of Rhodesian prehistory who have helped to throw light upon the culture sequence are Fathers Gardener and Stapleton, while a number of different workers have collected material from the famous site of the Victoria Falls, which is partly in Northern and partly in Southern Rhodesia.

Material representing—typologically—the great Chelleo-Acheulean culture has been found at many widely distributed points in Southern Rhodesia, among which especial mention may be made of the older gravels at Saw Mills, Gwelo Kopje, and the Bambata Cave.

At the last-named site Armstrong, during his excavations in 1929, discovered an Acheulean horizon which was overlain by a series of later cultures, thus yielding excellent evidence of the relative age of the Acheulean stage of culture in Southern Rhodesia. The results of the work at Bambata Cave—which I was privileged to visit while

Armstrong was carrying out this work there—have been published in the *Journal of the Royal Anthropological Institute*.[1] The Acheulean horizon yielded both cleavers and hand-axes comparable to the Upper Stellenbosch of South Africa, and this horizon was overlain by one which yielded what is described as a 'Mousterian' industry. This typologically compares closely with what I *formerly* termed 'Upper Mousterian' in East Africa, but now call 'developed Levalloisian'.

This 'Mousterian' or developed Levalloisian level had two intercalated levels which yielded an entirely different culture, comparable to a late Capsian or Aurignacian. This very interesting fact demonstrates that in Southern Rhodesia, as in East Africa, the makers of these two entirely different cultures were living contemporaneously in the same district, and it is also very interesting to note that, as in East Africa, the result of this contact was the evolution of a new culture showing elements of both the others. To this new culture which was found at Bambata in the occupational level immediately overlying the 'Mousterian', Armstrong has given the name of the Bambata culture. Three distinct stages of evolution of this culture were found, which are described as Lower, Middle, and Upper respectively.

Although the Bambata culture is of local evolution it is so like the Stillbay of East and South Africa that it might well have been named the Rhodesian Stillbay. The Lower Bambata stage is entirely comparable to what in East Africa I term Proto-Stillbay, while the Middle and Upper stages are the equivalent of the Lower and Upper Stillbay of East Africa. The type tools are beautifully made triangular and leaf-shaped points, commonly worked

[1] *Journal of the Royal Anthropological Institute*, vol. lxi, Jan.–June 1931.

all over both faces by careful pressure flaking technique, and with these points are associated burins, scrapers, and occasional backed blades and microliths.

Overlying the Upper Bambata horizon was one which yielded abundant Wilton material, so that the sequence demonstrated at Bambata Cave is that given in the two following tables, one of which is in Armstrong's terminology and the other in mine for comparison with East Africa.

Wilton	Wilton
Upper Bambata	Upper Rhodesian Stillbay
Middle Bambata	Lower Rhodesian Stillbay
Lower Bambata	Rhodesian-Proto Stillbay
contemporary { Neanthropic culture Mousterian }	an 'Aurignacian' phase Developed Levalloisian } contemporary
Acheulean	Acheulean

Of great importance are Neville Jones's recent excavations at Nswatugi and Madiliyangwa.

At the former, Neville Jones found a horizon yielding what he calls an Upper Bambata culture but which, as he says, is more developed than the Upper Bambata culture of Bambata itself. From the illustrations and the description of the assemblage found there I should say without hesitation that a culture stage, which in East Africa we should call Magosian, is represented. In addition to this, the Wilton of Nswatugi and Madiliyangwa seems to be rather different from the Wilton of Bambata Cave and possibly represents a rather later stage.

Judging by illustrations and descriptions an industry from a surface site at Saw Mills can also be attributed, on typological grounds, to the Magosian culture. Writing of this Saw Mills assemblage Neville Jones says *inter alia*: 'When the Saw Mills industry was first described it was impossible in the absence of any knowledge of related culture to suggest its position in the cultural sequence, but a study of it with the knowledge we now have of the Bambata culture and the Wilton industry make it very evident that the Wilton was derived from it.' Thus, to the table given above we can add Rhodesian Magosian between Upper Bambata and Wilton, and we can also add an Upper Wilton.

The derivation of the Rhodesian form of the Wilton culture from the Rhodesian Magosian shows that the former should be compared with the Wilton B of East Africa and not Wilton A, which is derived from the Upper Aurignacian direct through the Elmenteitan.

Another important site which has yielded magnificent Wilton and Bambata assemblages is Gokamere, and similar sites are now being recorded all over Southern Rhodesia.

Following the Wilton culture in Rhodesia comes a true Neolithic with polished axes, but this culture requires a great deal more study before its typical forms are known.

I have made no mention so far of a culture described by Neville Jones as the Hope Fountain culture, from a site not far from Bulawayo. Much of the material from Hope Fountain has a very primitive appearance, and probably represents a very early culture which was possibly contemporary with the hand-axe culture. But at the Hope Fountain site there is evidence of the presence of several cultural stages all mixed up together, and I shall not feel satisfied about the 'Hope Fountain culture' until it has been found under good stratigraphical conditions.[1]

I have also so far not discussed the Victoria Falls site, although I have mentioned it; that is because it belongs in part to Northern Rhodesia, and, in fact, the richest part

---

[1] Evidence collected by Neville Jones and A. L. Armstrong from the Victoria Falls is considered by them to support a high antiquity for the so-called Hope Fountain culture.

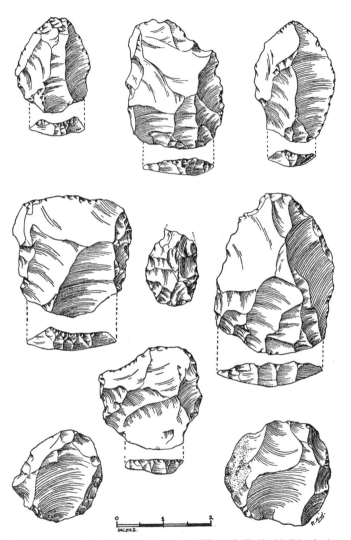

INCHES.

FIG. 17. Levalloisian assemblage from Victoria Falls, N. Rhodesia

of the site is on the Northern Rhodesian side of the
Zambesi River. The Victoria Falls site is of particular
importance because of the geological evidence which it
affords of the comparatively high antiquity of the Levalloisian culture in this region. The gravels which contain
the Levalloisian material, and also implements of the hand-
axe culture (which are usually more heavily rolled and
patinated), were laid down before the Gorge below the
Victoria Falls had been cut back to its present position,
and as the implementiferous gravels extend for several
miles downstream below the present position of the Falls
it is clear that the Gorge has been cut back for a considerable distance since the time when the makers of the
Levalloisian culture were living on its banks. Even if we
suppose that there have been pluvial periods during which
erosion was more rapid than to-day, a very considerable
period of time must be allowed, and we may safely say
that the Levalloisian culture, examples of which are found
in abundance in the gravels, dates back to very early times.
It is very regrettable, indeed, that there is as yet no positive
evidence from a fossil fauna which will help to compare
the date with that established for the Levalloisian culture
in East Africa, which we know was present before the end
of the Middle Pleistocene in East Africa (cf. Upper beds
at Oldoway).

There is some evidence of implements of Stillbay type
occurring also in the Victoria Falls gravels, but from the
evidence available to me I am rather inclined to think that
the specimens from the Victoria Falls gravels which have
been referred to the Stillbay culture, are really representa-
tives of the much earlier Pseudo-Stillbay culture which
I have already described from East Africa.

In his book, *South Africa's Past in Stone and Paint*, Mr.
Burkitt says, in reference to the collection which he made

at the Victoria Falls, 'typical coups-de-point occur, together with flakes trimmed all over the top and showing
occasionally a faceted prepared platform'. My own experience and that of others is that a very high percentage of
the flakes show prepared faceted platforms, and a series
of these is illustrated from a collection made by Miss M.
Nicol. More typically Levalloisian material would be hard
to find anywhere.

Apart from the Victoria Falls, Northern Rhodesia has
yielded very little Stone Age material of note. The famous
Broken Hill mine from which the skull of *Homo Rhodesiensis* was obtained, contained a number of Stone Age
horizons,[1] but we know very little of what they contained.
In 1929 I collected material from the dumps of cave-earth
which were dug out in the course of earlier mining operations, and this collection includes both Wilton and
Levalloisian specimens, so that I presume that levels
representing both these cultures were formerly present,
but more than that cannot be said.

In 1926 Mr. F. B. Macrae published a note on the Stone
Age in Northern Rhodesia,[2] and he partially excavated
a cave at Mumbwa which yielded in its lower levels some
hand-axes associated with round stone balls.

In the extreme north, near the shores of Lake Tanganyika at Abercorn, Solomon and I found in 1929 traces
of old lake terraces, from one of which we obtained a hand-
axe, while on the shores of the lake we found shell-mounds
with a Wilton industry exactly comparable to that found
in the shell-mounds on the shores of Victoria Nyanza.
Nyasaland, apart from some pre-Chellean implements

[1] 'An African occurrence of fossil mammalia associated with Stone
Implements. F. P. Mennel and E. C. Chubb in *Geol. Mag.* 1907,
p. 443.
[2] *Nada*, the Southern Rhodesian Native Affairs Department
Annual, 1926.

from fossiliferous deposits in the North, has, so far as I can ascertain, yielded very little Stone Age material except from scattered surface sites. Judged, however, from its geographical position, Nyasaland is certain to have many rich sites awaiting discovery.

We must now turn northwards to Somaliland and Abyssinia. Somaliland has yielded quantities of Stone Age implements to a number of collectors, including Seton Kerr, Barrington Brown, and T. Curle, but as yet we have no evidence of the age of any of these finds except from a study of the typology. This line of inquiry suggests that many stages of the hand-axe culture, as well as the Levalloisian, Aurignacian, and Stillbay cultures, are present. In addition to this, some Wilton and Neolithic material has also been found, but not in great quantity.

Abyssinia has so far yielded very little material, although there are a few collections which include both Neolithic polished axes as well as typologically earlier material from the region.

The only important Abyssinian site is the rock-shelter at Diri-Daoua, where Father Teilhard carried out an excavation and recovered an industry which is described by Professor Breuil as *une évolution particulière du Moustérien évolué*. The assemblage includes flakes with faceted striking platforms, cores, occasional scrapers, and large numbers of points, some of them resembling true Mousterian points and others trimmed all over both surfaces and suggesting minute hand-axes, with occasional leaf-shaped specimens. From this description it would seem as though this industry from Diri-Daoua was very similar indeed to that which I have termed Pseudo-Stillbay in East Africa, examples of which are figured in Chapter III.

In his recent study of the Pleistocene geology of the Rift Valley lakes in Abyssinia, Dr. Erik Nilsson found a

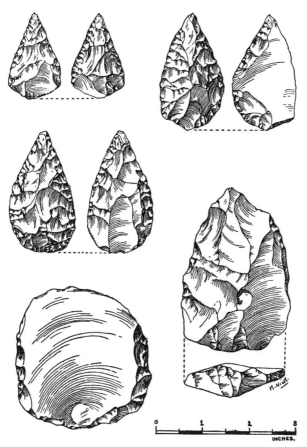

FIG. 18. A series from a surface collection from British Somaliland, indicating the presence of the Stillbay culture (Cambridge
Collection)

K

certain number of some implements, but, so far as I know, these have not yet been studied. I understand that in some cases the specimens were found under conditions which will make it possible to date them, and, in consequence, the publication of the material is awaited with interest.

At the north end of Lake Rudolph is the valley of the Omo River. Here there are extensive fossil beds which yield a fauna comparable to that from Oldoway, but so far no stone implements have been found in these beds. I am, however, confident that somewhere in the Omo region Stone Age material comparable to that from Oldoway will one day be found.

It is exceedingly unfortunate that at present we have so little accurate information about the Stone Age in the two areas just mentioned, the Somalilands (British, French, and Italian) and Abyssinia, because this whole area is one of extreme importance for the elucidation of a number of problems relating to the prehistory of Africa as a whole.

We have already seen in the chapter on the changes of geography in Stone Age times that there is reason to believe that the Red Sea did not exist in its present form during the earlier part of the Stone Age, and that there is a likelihood that there were at least land-bridges in this region linking Africa with Arabia. The chapter on the fauna of the Stone Age yielded additional evidence supporting this view because we saw that many of the now extinct animals found in Africa during Lower and Middle Pleistocene times belong to Asiatic groups of animals, which occur as fossils in North India (cf. the fossil buffaloes, giant sheep, the antlered giraffids, &c.).

In addition to this geographical and faunal evidence we know that in India Stone Age cultures very similar to those of Africa are to be found, so that from all points of view there is reason to link Africa and south-western Asia in early Stone Age times. This being so we naturally look to the Somaliland area on the one hand and the deserts of Arabia on the other, to give us evidence which will bridge the gap between North India and East Africa. Owing to political as well as to climatic factors it is doubtful if we shall get much information about the Stone Age in Arabia for a long time to come, so that it is from the Somali-Abyssinian area that we must hope for information. Here is a very fruitful field of research for some one with the necessary qualifications to carry out such an investigation, and it is to be hoped that before long an attempt will be made to study this area.

Another area which is geographically of great importance to the prehistorian is the Sudan, together with western Abyssinia. At present we have absolutely no means of linking up the very rich prehistoric field in East Africa with the Nile Valley in Egypt, and yet the Nile rises in East Africa, and it seems highly probable that that part of the Nile Valley which passes through the Sudan will yield the very information that we so badly need.

At present, apart from a good deal of material which apparently belongs to the Neolithic period, and a few rare sites where surface finds of implements—which typologically belong to earlier cultures—have been recorded, the Sudan is a blank from the point of view of Stone Age cultures.

Even the Neolithic material yet awaits detailed publication. Among the exhibits in the Wellcome Historical Medical Museum when it was at Wigmore Street, I saw Neolithic material from Gebel Moya which very strongly recalled the Njoroan Neolithic culture of East Africa, and this resemblance was increased by the fact that, as in Kenya, it was associated with full-length burials in

cemeteries; but, although the excavations at Gebel Moya
were carried out many years ago, no detailed account of
the discoveries has appeared.

From the Sudan we pass to the Congo; lying as it does
on the borders of Uganda Protectorate, which is yielding
such plentiful Stone Age material, we might expect that
at least in its eastern borders it would also have much
Stone Age material. At present, however, there is little
evidence of Stone Age cultures occurring in the Congo
region except in Neolithic times.

There are many places in the western part of the Congo
that are likely to provide rich finds of early Stone Age
material, with a distinct possibility that it will be associated
with a fossil fauna. The western shores of Lakes Albert,
Edward, Tanganyika, and Mweru all lie in the Congo,
and they are almost certain to have ancient lake beaches
containing stone implements and fossils, under conditions
which would make dating possible.

The more forested regions of the Congo are perhaps
less likely to yield Stone Age material belonging to the
earlier cultures, as it seems likely that this region has been
under dense forest throughout the Pleistocene period, and,
on the whole, Stone Age man preferred more or less open
country.

The best-known Stone Age site in the Congo is Tumba
and its immediate surroundings which have yielded collections of stone implements to a number of different
people. Some have regarded the Tumbian culture, as it
is called, as a comparatively early culture which shows
affinities with the great hand-axe culture, but the work
of Dr. Jacques describing the material found by Haas
does not in the least support this view.

It is possible—nay, probable—that there are several
stages of the Tumbian culture, but the fact that polished

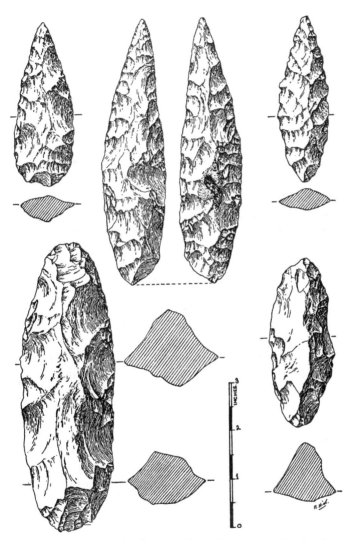

FIG. 19. Tumbian implements from the type station in the
Congo (British Museum Collection)

axes and well-made arrow-heads are usually found with the more typical Tumbian implements, seems to point to a Neolithic age for the whole of the Tumbian.

Assemblages of implements which have been assigned to the Tumbian culture have been found at a number of widely separated points in the Belgian and French Congo, and the Tumbian culture is also undoubtedly represented in Uganda and Kenya. The best Tumbian material which I have yet seen from East Africa is that in the collections made by Archdeacon Owen to the north-east of Victoria Nyanza, and I have myself collected similar material in that region. Unfortunately, as we have already seen, there is no direct evidence in East Africa which will show its relationship to the other Neolithic cultures.

In a typical Tumbian assemblage, leaf-shaped points worked all over both faces and sometimes of considerable size, are associated with arrow-heads of various types including 'tranchet' forms, polished axes, and large and rather clumsy implements with resemblances to the so-called 'picks' found in Europe.

A series of implements from Tumba, the type site, are illustrated in this chapter, but neither arrow-heads nor polished axes are shown, as the collection from which these specimens are illustrated (in the British Museum) does not include either of these forms.

A collection of Tumbian material from Kenya is also shown for purposes of comparison. It should be noted that superficially some of the leaf-shaped points of the Tumbian culture resemble those found in the Stillbay culture, but if an assemblage is found there is no fear of any confusion arising from this similarity.

From the Congo we turn to Nigeria and the Gold Coast, and there again we find that there is extraordinarily little information available concerning the Stone Age

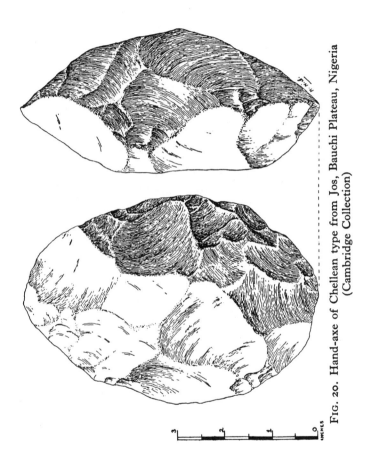

FIG. 20. Hand-axe of Chellean type from Jos, Bauchi Plateau, Nigeria
(Cambridge Collection)

cultures, although surface finds as well as discoveries of implements in alluvial deposits show that apparently various early Stone Age cultures occur, in addition to much Neolithic material. In a paper published by the Geological Survey of Nigeria, Mr. J. H. Braunholz, of the British Museum, has described and illustrated specimens collected in the Jos district of the Bauchi Plateau. Another collection from the same region is in the Museum of Archaeology and Ethnology at Cambridge.

From typological evidence it seems as though several stages of the great hand-axe culture are to be found in Nigeria as well as typical Levalloisian material, but on typological evidence alone little can be said. Recently the British Museum has acquired some very nicely made microliths, suggesting a Wilton type of culture, from Wana, near the Bauchi Plateau; these are apparently the first microliths to be found in Nigeria. There is also a very great deal of material—apparently attributable to a Neolithic culture—to be found in Nigeria. Polished axes, as well as long stone chisels, are common, and some of them apparently were in use long after metal was introduced.

Members of the Geological Survey of the Gold Coast have collected a considerable number of stone implements, and their collections are housed in that Survey's headquarters in London. No detailed study of the material has, so far as I know, been published.

We have now briefly examined the Stone Age cultures found all over Africa, and must pass on to other aspects of prehistory in that continent. Before doing so, however, it will be convenient if the sum total of what we know is summarized in the table which follows.

Painting of a Kudu at the Rock Shelter of Nswatugi, Matopos Hills, South Rhodesia. Colour, dark brownish-red

CHAPTER VIII

STONE AGE ART IN AFRICA

FOR many years cave paintings and rock engravings, which are found in many parts of South Africa and Southern Rhodesia, had attracted the attention of both travellers and scientists, but there was very little evidence which could be used to date any of this art. It was well known that when the European first arrived in South Africa the Bushmen were still living a Stone Age life, using stone implements (probably of Wilton and Smithfield type), and it was also known that these Bushmen had been in the habit of painting upon the walls of the caves and rock shelters which they inhabited. In consequence it had become customary in South Africa to describe all these rock paintings as 'Bushman paintings' and to ascribe them all to a very late date.

In 1928 Mr. Burkitt published an account of his brief survey of the Stone Age in South Africa under the title of *South Africa's Past in Stone and Paint*, and in this book he showed for the first time that the cave paintings and engravings of South Africa were quite obviously not all of the same age, and he suggested that probably some of the art was of considerable antiquity. Burkitt pointed out that there were a number of quite distinct styles of painting to be found in Southern Rhodesia, and that in addition to the stylistic differences it was very noticeable that the different styles were, for the most part, carried out in different colouring matter. After critically examining a number of sites and studying the cases of superposition which were found, Burkitt arrived at the following conclusion concerning the art in Southern Rhodesia. 'This makes altogether five age periods that can with safety be

determined, but it is perhaps simpler to think in terms
of three groups; an early pre-dark-claret one, a middle
one composed only of the dark-claret series, and a later
one including the earthy yellow and white series and
apparently leading up to and consummated in the polychrome series.'

In 1928, after the South African meeting of the British
Association, Professor Breuil visited Southern Rhodesia
and examined the paintings at a number of sites. He considers that the sequence given by Burkitt is incomplete.
The oldest paintings of all are, according to him, a black
series; next comes a series usually in white, after which
are the yellows and reds of Burkitt's pre-dark-claret series.
The suggestion that there is a black series older than all
the other paintings in Southern Rhodesia was confirmed
by a recent examination by Miss M. Nicol, who noted a
similar sequence to that given by Professor Breuil.

At a site called Makumbi and elsewhere, Burkitt found
that a yellow series of paintings and a bright red one were
both earlier than the dark claret series, from the point of
view of superpositions, but the relationship of the bright
red and the yellow series to each other was not clear. At
Bambata the yellow series is always under the bright red
series, showing that it was apparently the older.

In 1929, a year after Burkitt had worked out this sequence of styles and colours in Southern Rhodesia,
Armstrong carried out his detailed excavation at Bambata
cave, and the result of his work, so far as it bears upon the
question of the art, may be summarized in his own words,
as follows:[1]

'In the middle and upper zones numerous specimens of
raw colouring material was found, consisting of balls and
fragments of yellow ochre, and pencils, fragments and balls

[1] See *J.R.A.I.*, vol. lxi, 1933, pp. 251 et seq.

of red and brown haematites and ochres. The pencils were pear-shaped or triangular in shape and invariably showed definite striae of the pointed ends and frequently upon their surfaces and edges also, obviously produced by rubbing on a gritty surface. Several of the broken fragments of ochre bear similar marks, but the balls of yellow ochre and most of the specimens of red ochre, being softer, have not always retained these striae although their shape is evidently artificial and upon some specimens there are flat surfaces which appear to have resulted from use. . . . A study of the technique of the wall painting shows that it was customary to draw the animals and figures first in outline, generally with a fairly bold line and that subsequently the body was filled in with colour. It is clear that the process of filling in was generally done by scouring the rock with the appropriate colour in the manner that a child uses crayons . . . therefore, strictly speaking, these are pastel drawings rather than paintings. The indications of use displayed are exactly such as would result from these processes and I have no doubt that in them we have some of the actual tools used in producing the paintings. This being so they provide an important link between the paintings and the artefacts which has hitherto been entirely lacking.

'Colouring material was distributed consistently in each layer of the Upper Bambata zone and down to the centre of the middle zone: the lower pieces . . . were at five feet and consisted of yellow balls of ochre. . . . Red ochre was not found lower than 3 ft. 6 inches, and the brown and red haematites were absent after the 2 ft. 6 inch level, though frequent between 6 inches and 2 ft. 6 inches.

'It will be observed that the colouring materials are in a stratified succession of yellow (lowest) red and brown and red, and it is significant that this succession is precisely that of the order of superposition of the wall paintings. The oldest paintings which are now almost entirely faded away were executed in yellow ochre and for a long period this colour appears to have been that in sole use. . . .

'In view of this close agreement between stratification of

colouring material and the order of the superposition of the
paintings, a correlation between the two seems to be reasonably
justified and the paintings, except for the latest series, can
safely be assigned to Middle and Upper Bambata times.'

I have quoted this report of Armstrong's at length because of its very great importance. Here we have positive
evidence that the men who were responsible for the earliest
paintings at Bambata cave (and presumably also at the
other caves where the earliest series occurs) were the
makers of the Middle and later stages of culture described
by Armstrong as the Bambata culture. We have already
seen that while the Lower Bambata compares more with
the Proto-Stillbay of East Africa, the Middle and Upper
stages are the Rhodesian equivalent of the East and South
African branches of the Stillbay culture.

At present we have, unfortunately, very little other evidence upon which we can rely for associating the Stillbay
culture with the earliest South African art, but at the same
time it is an important fact that the areas where *early*
paintings occur are chiefly areas where the so-called
Middle Stone Age group of cultures are also found.

Another important fact in connexion with the evidence
from Bambata is that the only human skull which as yet
can be almost certainly associated with the Stillbay culture
is the Fishhoek skull, from Peers cave in South Africa.
This skull, which has been reported upon by Sir Arthur
Keith, represents an ancestor of the later day Bushmen
of South Africa. We know that these later Bushmen had
many of them considerable artistic ability, and it thus is
possible that most of the art of South Africa and Rhodesia
is attributable to the Bushman race, although at different
periods of time. There is no doubt at all that, although
some of the art is early, other examples are of recent origin,
for some of the scenes depict domestic animals, such as

oxen, and others show what appear to be Europeans wearing hats.

A number of important works illustrating the cave paintings of South Africa and Rhodesia have been published and those who wish to get a clear idea of the nature of this art cannot do better than consult such works as Miss Tongue's *Bushman Paintings*, Mr. Burkitt's book which has already been mentioned,[1] and the notes by Professor Breuil published after his visit in 1929.

Recently, too, Professor Leo Frobenius and a party of artists have made an extensive study of South African art and some of this has been illustrated in *Cahiers d'Art*.[2]

In the Union of South Africa a very great deal of the art is undoubtedly late in time, and the very beautiful polychrome paintings which are so common are almost certainly to be attributed to the people who made the later stages of the Wilton culture; in other words, they are probably the work of the immediate ancestors of the Bushmen who were in the country at the time of the coming of the white men.

In his examination of the South African paintings Professor Breuil came to the conclusion that there are 'at least 16 pictorial series'. The first eight of these are the early and true Stone Age ones, for, but from the ninth onwards, the paintings show cattle and also Bantu natives and Europeans. This does not mean, however, that they were not the work of Bushmen who were still living a more or less Stone Age life. Only a few of the styles found in Southern Rhodesia reoccur, and the earliest black ones are missing. The eighth series, which is the last truly

[1] *Bushmen Paintings*, by Helen Tongue, Oxford University Press, 1909; *South Africa's Past in Stone and Paint*, by M. C. Burkitt, Cambridge University Press, 1928.
[2] *Cahiers d'Art*, Paris, 1931.

Stone Age one from Breuil's point of view, is that characterized by the best polychrome paintings.

In a good many cases these polychrome paintings of the
Union are seen to overlie semi-obliterated claret coloured
paintings, suggesting that an older claret series comparable
to the claret series of Southern Rhodesia is present. Even
in the polychrome series it is possible to trace several distinct stages, and the later stages show a marked falling off
in artistic merit in most cases, thus suggesting that
degeneration had set in.

According to Mr. Burkitt a painted scene near Molteno,
in which white men with wide-brimmed hats are figured,
belongs to this late degenerate period, suggesting that
by the time the white men came to South Africa the art
of the Bushmen was already much degenerated. Even if
this be true, the fact remains that when Europeans first
came to South Africa the Bushmen, who were still really
a Stone Age people surviving into modern times, were still
practising cave art, and it is a great pity that in those early
days of colonization no one took the trouble to find out
and record either the methods employed in making these
paintings or the reasons why the painting was done at all.

The latter question is one on which there is much
controversy. Some people hold that all cave art was of a
magical and semi-religious nature, and there is a good deal
of evidence to show that some of the art certainly had a
magical and religious significance.

It is probable that scenes which show male and female
animals in pairs had something to do with fertility rites.
On the other hand, many scenes seem to be much more
purely pictorial, and probably the truth is that art was
practised both for art's sake and also sometimes for magical
purposes.

Human beings are very commonly figured in the South

African and Rhodesian paintings, and usually they are far less naturalistically drawn than are the animals in the same style. At the same time the artists were often at pains to emphasize—almost to the point of caricature—such characteristics as steatopyga.

In certain regions of South Africa paintings are replaced by engravings and, in the words of Burkitt, the 'distribution coincides more or less with an area rich in dolerite, the rock upon which most of the engravings are usually made'. Other rocks are sometimes found to have been engraved as well, and in Southern Rhodesia a few examples of engravings on granite have been found.

Miss M. Nicol, who recently spent some time examining some of the rock-shelters with paintings in Southern Rhodesia, tells me that at one shelter in the Umvukwes district, where there were many paintings of the yellow and red series, there are also some engravings which include a zebra and several other animals. Unfortunately the engravings and paintings were upon different parts of the rock surface, so that there was no way of determining their relative ages.

In the engravings of South Africa a number of distinct styles have been noted, and Burkitt divides the engravings into four groups of different ages. In the oldest group he places engravings which show 'a fine incised outline' while the bodies of the animals are 'filled in with fine lines more or less parallel to this outline'.

In the second group the figures of the animals are 'made by a pocking technique without any definite outline; sometimes there is merely an outline formed by a more or less wide band of coarse pockings; sometimes the whole of the body of the animal, sometimes the head and neck only, are covered with pock-marks'.

In both of these series the surface of the rock upon

which the engravings have been made often shows that it
has weathered very considerably since the artists were at
work, thus suggesting that they are far from being very
recent. Because of this weathering, too, the figures of
these two series are often comparatively hard to see.

At the very well-known site called Afvallingskop near
Koffiefontein in the Orange Free State, Miss Nicol
discovered last year a particularly interesting figure (belonging to the second series) which had apparently been
overlooked by previous workers as it does not seem to
have been recorded. This remarkable figure is repro-
duced in this chapter for the first time. It represents
a man wearing a pair of antelope horns on his head
and with a long tail like a lion's. Such human figures in
'fancy dress', although by no means unknown, are rare in
Stone Age art. One of the classic examples is the 'masked
man' or 'sorcerer' from Trois Frères in the South of
France, and there are also two or three paintings of
masked men among the published material from South
Africa.

In her beautifully illustrated work on *The Rock engraving of Griqualand West and Bechuanaland, South
Africa*, Miss M. Wilman shows one masked man with
the comment, 'Man, masked, with a tail, a very unusual
representation'.

Both engraved, the masked man found by Miss Nicol
and that published by Miss Wilman, are noticeable for
having a line cutting across the penis, the significance of
which is not at all clear.

Similar lines cutting across the penis are to be found in
some of the painted representations of men both in
Southern Rhodesia and the Union, suggesting that some
definite significance must have been attached to this sign,
and also suggesting that some of the paintings and en-

gravings were the work of the same race, or at least
people with a similar custom.

Describing the third series of engravings, Burkitt says
that it is

'the most important and most frequently seen of all, and
judging from the fact that the patina (or weathering of the
engraved surfaces) is sometimes fairly deep and sometimes
very slight, it must have lasted through a long period of time.
. . . Engravings of this series show a clear outline, the body of
the animal being, as it were, deeply rubbed all over. That
this "rubbing" was done with a fine punch making a minute
pocking all over the surface seems to me to be proved by the
fact that definite pock-marks can occasionally be made out.'

The final series of engravings noted by Burkitt is not
of importance to us as they are made with a metal knife
and do not belong to the Stone Age at all.

In addition to the four series noted by Burkitt and
summarized above, we may add a fifth, which in style of
drawing as well as in technique is quite distinct. The
figures of this series are very faint indeed, and apparently
very old; they underlie figures belonging to series one and
two and are certainly older. The animals are represented
by a simple incised outline only. It might be argued that
these were unfinished examples of Burkitt's first series,
but this idea is negatived by the fact that the artistic style
is quite distinct and much more naturalistic. Professor
Breuil places these in a group by themselves and regards
them as the oldest, this view being confirmed by further
discoveries made by Miss Nicol.

One of the most striking differences between the Stone
Age art of South Africa and of Europe is the fact that in
the latter there are very many examples of beautiful engravings upon small stones, and upon rough pieces of bone
and antler, as well as upon artefacts made of bone and

L

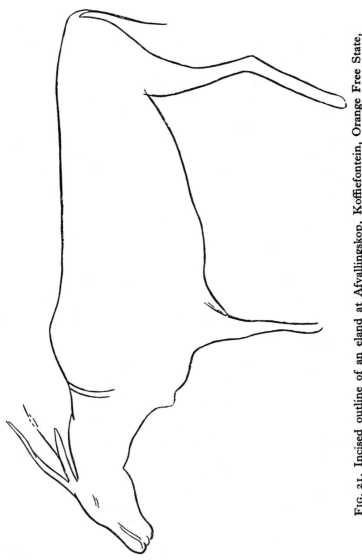

FIG. 21. Incised outline of an eland at Afvallingskop, Koffiefontein, Orange Free State, representing style 1 of the South African engravings. Reduced to ½ (approx.)

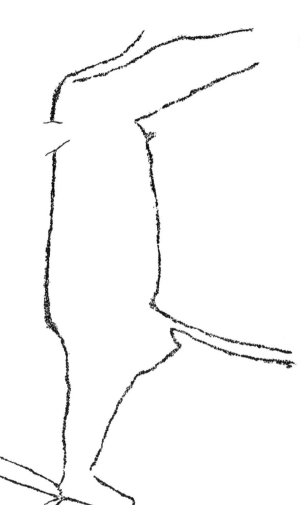

FIG. 22. An eland in which the outline is 'pocked' instead of incised, representing either an early phase of style 3 or an unfinished example. (Equals Burkitt's style 2). From Afvallingskop. Reduced to $\frac{1}{5}$ (approx.)

FIG. 23. A masked human figure in style 3 (from Afvallingskop)
Reduced to ½ (approx.)

FIG. 24. A frieze of animals and ostriches belonging to a late stage of style 3 (from Afvallingskop). Reduced to $\frac{1}{5}$ (approx.)

antler and ivory, while in South Africa the finding of
engraved or painted objects actually in the archaeological
deposits is very rare indeed. The most notable exception
to this in South Africa is to be found in connexion with
burials of the 'Strand-loopers' or shell-mound peoples.
In several instances burials belonging to these people have
revealed upon excavation the interesting fact that the
bodies had large flat pebbles and broken stone mortars
placed upon them at burial, and that upon these stones
were painted conventionalized human and animal forms.

The summary of Stone Age art in South Africa and
Rhodesia which I have given above is very incomplete,
chiefly because I have not seen more than a very few
examples of this art myself, and I do not feel qualified
to give more than a brief summary based upon what I
have read.

From South Africa we must now go northwards to
East Africa and thence to North Africa.

The first discovery of any form of cave art in East
Africa seems to have been made in 1908 by some mis-
sionaries working at Buanja, near Bukoba on the western
shores of Victoria Nyanza. Some rock-shelters were
found in which there were numerous conventionalized
human figures in red. These were shown to the members
of the Duke of Mecklenburg's scientific expedition in
June of that year, and were subsequently described by
the ethnologist of the Expedition, Dr. Czekanowski.

So far as I know, no further discovery was made until
after the War, when in 1923 Mr. F. B. Bagshawe published a note in *Man* under the heading of 'Rock Paintings
of the Kangeju Bushmen, Tanganyika Territory', in which
he described some paintings from the area lying to the
west of Lake Eyassi.

Following this in 1929 Mr. T. A. M. Nash published

PLATE VI

The Rock Shelter at Kisese in Tanganyika Territory, where some of the cave-paintings were found. The rhinoceroses in Fig. 26 and the antelopes in Plate VIII are from this site

a short paper in the *Journal of the Royal Anthropological Institute* in which he gave an illustrated account of some paintings found on the walls of rock-shelters in the Kondoa Irangi province of Tanganyika Territory. Describing them, Nash says: 'Most of them are in a rather bad state of preservation and in many of the places where they have been kept in the best condition they are spoilt by the jumble and chaos of drawing superimposed upon drawing. The pigment used in every case is red, sometimes of rather an orange colour and sometimes purplish.' In other words, Nash had found a site where there were a number of superpositions and where several different coloured pigments had been used.

On our way by lorry to South Africa in 1929 my companions and I called on Mr. Nash, and he very kindly took us to see some of his sites and also told us how to get to others. Although we had no time to do any detailed work it was perfectly obvious that there were a number of different styles represented and that a great deal of careful study would be necessary to elucidate the sequence of the styles, and I made a resolution that I would revisit the area at some future occasion and spend some time on this fascinating work. In 1935 the opportunity came, and I spent two weeks making a preliminary examination, the results of which will be given in brief presently. Besides re-examining Nash's sites we located several others, and were thus able to get some idea of the sequence of the styles by checking off one site with another.

In 1931 Mr. A. R. Culwick published a paper in the *Journal of the Anthropological Institute* on some more paintings from Central Tanganyika. In this paper he pointed out that the superpositions in the examples which he had found gave the following results. 'We have the line drawings as the earliest series, the paintings in plain colour as the most recent, while those with a dark culture occupy an intermediate position.' Unfortunately, at the sites found by Culwick no complete line-drawing of an animal remains; in other words, the oldest series seen by him was already very nearly obliterated.

In none of the cases from East Africa cited above is there any proof that the paintings described belong to the Stone Age, but I have little doubt that some of the earlier ones figured by Nash and Culwick were painted by a Stone Age people. The more recent ones, however, are almost certainly very much later and are possibly the work of comparatively recent Bantu tribes.

A detailed account of the results of the work which I did in 1935 will be published elsewhere, but a summary must be given here as it gives a more complete idea of the sequence of styles than anything previously published from East Africa, and makes a very interesting comparison with some of the Rhodesian and South African art.

Seven different sites were carefully examined, and between them they yielded the following sequence of styles:

(1) The earliest to be found are figures of animals in red and in every case the whole figure is coloured, except for the face, which is drawn in thick outline only and the middle left blank. Where the animal had a mane it is shown by a series of short dashes.

(2) Very curious human figures in an unusual purple colour, rather badly drawn animals in the same purple, and large areas of concentric rings of dots apparently drawn with the finger tip dipped in the colouring material.

(Note: the relationship of (1) and (2) is not absolutely clear, but both groups are older than any of the others, which, in all cases of superposition, are over them).

(3) A number of figures in which ostriches and giraffes predominate, drawn in outline in a purplish red; the

PLATE VII

Tracing cave-paintings at Cheke Rock Shelter in Tanganyika Territory. Note : The white surrounding some of the paintings had been applied by a previous visitor to enable him to take photographs. Part of the frieze shown in the frontispiece is seen here

PLATE VIII

Paintings of antelopes (?) in style I at Kisese Rock Shelter, Tanganyika Territory (from a tracing). Reduced to ¼ (approx.)

PLATE IX

Group of human figures and an elephant (?) surrounded by
interrupted lines, at Cheke Rock Shelter, Tanganyika Territory. These paintings are in style 7 (from a tracing)
Reduced to $\frac{1}{8}$ (approx.)

technique of applying the colouring material was different from that in style (5) (in which also the drawings are even more naturalistic) but at the same time style (3) seems to be related to (5) and is probably only a little earlier than it.

(4) A few very indistinct black outline-figures are always under style (5) and seem to come in here. They may possibly belong to style (3), but the difference in colour as well as an improvement in style suggests that they should be classed alone.

(5) In this style the art is at its best. Figures of animals are drawn in outline with very thin lines of paint. The animals are very naturalistic and details such as sex organs, manes, &c., are very carefully shown. The colour used is a claret-red.

(6) Some curious yellow and orange human figures and animals rather badly drawn are found overlying animals in style (5) and underlying style (7) so that they are placed here. They are comparatively rare, and not to be confused with the much later orange and yellow figures.

(7) This style consists of animals in a dark claret-red colour in which the whole body is coloured. The animals are sufficiently naturalistic to be easily recognizable, but the detail is not good. Sex organs are not shown, nor are the manes of giraffes, &c. Animals in this style are common. There are a few human figures which may belong to this group but which were not found under conditions which gave any direct proof of this.

(8) Overlying style (7) at several sites are animals drawn in a thick red outline. These animals are not nearly as naturalistic as those of stage (5), and the commonest animals figured are elephants. In one case an elephant in this style is nearly 10 feet long and 5 feet high. The wrinkles on the trunks of the elephants are always carefully shown, although little attention is paid to other details.

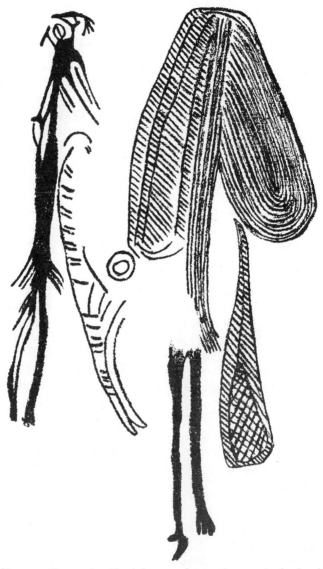

FIG. 25. Conventionalized human figures in purple (style 2)
(from Kisese Rock-Shelter No. 2, Tanganyika Territory).
Reduced to $\frac{1}{4}$ (approx.)

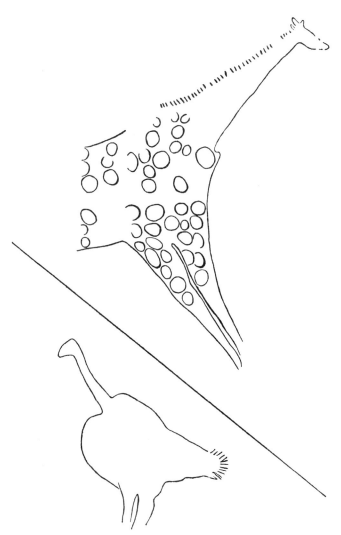

Fig. 26. Painting in style 3 (purplish-red outline) [from Kisese Rock-Shelter No. 1 (ostrich) and Rock-Shelter No. 2 (giraffe)]. Reduced to $\frac{1}{8}$ (approx.)

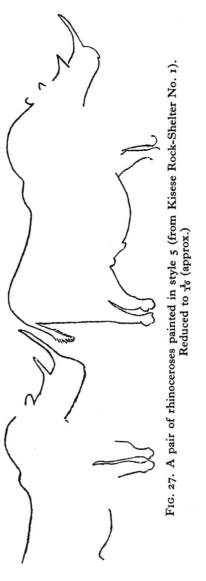

Fig. 27. A pair of rhinoceroses painted in style 5 (from Kisese Rock-Shelter No. 1). Reduced to $\frac{1}{16}$ (approx.)

FIG. 28. An animal in a very curious style which cannot at present be placed in the sequence (from Kisese Rock-Shelter No. 2). Reduced to $\frac{1}{8}$ (approx.)

(9) A series of animals drawn in outline in a brick-red colour. Very stiff and conventionalized drawing quite unlike any of the earlier outline styles. Often the tails of animals are omitted.

(10) A series of very curious orange human figures and badly drawn animals in solid colour.

(11) Figures in a dirty yellow and dirty white, apparently very recent indeed, including white hands.

(12) Orange coloured lines and hands.

(13) Black human figures very conventionalized indeed. The last three groups are very recent and are probably not of Stone Age date at all. In addition to this series of thirteen distinct superimposed styles, several other styles were noted, but no evidence was found to show where in the sequence they belonged. A great deal more work remains to be done, and this it is intended to do if possible during the next season's work.

At present we have no positive evidence at all that any of the paintings are the work of Stone Age man, although on analogy with Rhodesia and South Africa it seems certain that the earlier ones are. Excavations will have to be carried out before positive proof can be obtained. It may be mentioned, however, that a Wilton culture certainly occurs in the top deposits of these shelters, and that there is evidence also of the presence in the district of a Stillbay culture. Until further work has been carried out no more than this can be said about prehistoric art in East Africa.

From East Africa we turn to North Africa, where there are a number of recorded sites with engravings or paintings. Of these, however, the vast majority are apparently of very recent origin from the prehistorian's point of view, and belong at the earliest to the Neolithic period, for they frequently include domestic animals, such as cattle. There are, however, a few sites where the available evidence sug-

PLATE X

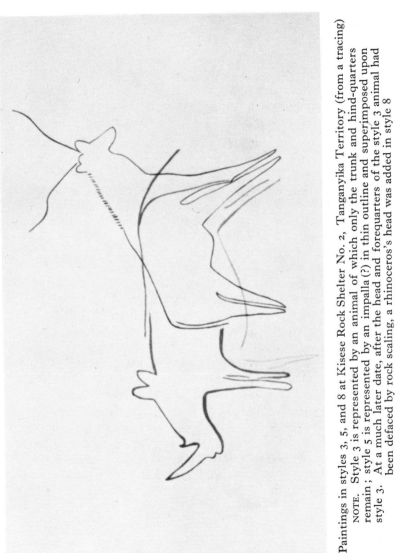

Paintings in styles 3, 5, and 8 at Kisese Rock Shelter No. 2, Tanganyika Territory (from a tracing)

NOTE. Style 3 is represented by an animal of which only the trunk and hind-quarters remain; style 5 is represented by an impalla (?) in thin outline and superimposed upon style 3. At a much later date, after the head and forequarters of the style 3 animal had been defaced by rock scaling, a rhinoceros's head was added in style 8

gests that we are dealing with an art which belongs to a more remote period. One of the most important of these sites is Djebel Owenat in the Lybian desert, an account of which was given by Prince Kemal el Dine and Professor Breuil in 1928. According to Breuil the engravings at Djebel Owenat can be divided into a number of distinct styles of different periods. Concerning the earliest of these Breuil says:[1]

'The oldest layer (of engravings) is of exactly the same style as the best rock-engravings of South Africa. It is impossible to distinguish any difference between the giraffes and ostriches of the two groups, which are in a remarkably good naturalistic style. The latter belong, according to the latest investigations, to a comparatively old geological period . . . and are associated with implements much older than the microliths of the Strandloopers and Bushmen. It is thus probable that the oldest group (at Djebel Owenat) can be assigned to a hunting people of the Upper Palaeolithic period.'

Subsequent to the work done by Prince Kemal el Dine, Djebel Owenat was visited by Count Almassy, who found a number of other sites, including several shelters, with magnificent paintings as distinct from engravings. These have not yet been published in detail, but they were partially illustrated in the *Illustrated London News*.

From the number of shelters with engravings and paintings at Djebel Owenat it is almost certain that if a careful and detailed scientific investigation was carried out there, we should learn a great deal about the culture stages of the people who were responsible for this art, but at present we have only indirect evidence—such as the fact that many of the animals represented are now no longer present in the area or are altogether extinct—to help us in dating this art.

[1] A free translation from the original in the article in *Revue Scientifique*, 1928.

Among other engravings which can be assigned without question to the Stone Age period in North Africa are many which were found at sites in South Oran. These have been described by Flamand, Frobenius, and Obermaier. There are two main groups of engravings in this region, an early one in which extinct animals and animals that no longer are found in North Africa occur, and a much later group where the engravings are associated with inscriptions. The latter do not concern us here. Among the best-known sites where engravings of the earlier group occur is Ksar-el-Amar, where there are magnificent engravings of gigantic buffaloes of the Bubalus group, and also of a rhinoceros, while other sites clearly show lions, elephants, and giraffes.

At one or two sites in North Africa a few small fragments of decorated ostrich egg-shell and other material have been found *in situ* in deposits containing human cultures. The most important of these is probably the painted and engraved fragment of an ostrich egg-shell cup found by Dr. Clergeau at El Mengoub. This was associated with a Capsian culture and it comes from a region where the walls of many rock-shelters show engravings. The animal represented on the egg-shell is a bovid and it was engraved in outline first and then covered with a red colouring material. On the walls of some of the rock-shelters of the region are similar engravings associated with colouring material so that this gives strong suggestive evidence that these engravings are also of Capsian origin.

Apart from this there is very little evidence in North Africa which tells us who the artists were, or what their stage of cultures was, and therefore, as in the case of East Africa, we can only say that a great deal more very careful scientific work needs to be carried out. Looking at the Stone Age art of Africa as a whole, we find that the vast majority of it can only be assigned to the Stone Age on very general grounds, and it is only a few sites such as Bambata which have yielded positive evidence which links certain artistic styles with definite cultural horizons.

One very big problem emerges from the study, and that is whether any real connexion can be said to exist between the Stone Age art of Europe and Africa. Many people believe that there is a direct connexion, and all kinds of supporting arguments have been put forward. The early Stone Age art of Europe was the work of the races that made the Aurignacian and Magdalenian cultures, and art appears in South Africa for the first time just when Aurignacian (or so-called Neanthropic) influences are first noted. In this connexion Armstrong wrote:

'It is noteworthy that the horizon upon which colouring material first occurred and which presumably marks the beginning of art in Southern Rhodesia, is the point at which a distinct improvement in the technique of burins was noticed and from which horizon upwards they were increasingly abundant. It is probable that the incoming of art and the improvement in burins were alike due to a new wave of Neanthropic people or influence from the north. If this correlation between the cave paintings and the Upper Palaeolithic culture of South Africa is reliable, as I believe it to be, it provides a further and highly important link between it and the Upper Aurignacian of Europe, and supports the evidence for a common origin for both in the region of the Sahara of North Africa.'

While I do not deny that the earlier Stone Age art of Africa and Europe may have a common source, I must say that I am more inclined to regard it as due to a quite independent growth of artistic ideas in the different regions. This will be further discussed in the concluding chapter of this book.

CHAPTER IX

STONE AGE MAN IN AFRICA

IN our examination of the Stone Age cultures which have been found all over Africa, we have seen that assemblages of implements belonging to the great hand-axe culture are very common over a great part of the continent, and in particular in South and East Africa as well as parts of North Africa. On the other hand, we have also seen that it is but rarely that associated fossil remains of animals have been found with this culture. This fact suggests that at many of the sites where implements of the Chelleo-Acheulean hand-axe culture have been found the necessary conditions for the fossilization and preservation of bone do not occur. In view of this it is hardly surprising that human remains representing the makers of this great culture in Africa are so little known.

Before we pass on to a discussion of such fragmentary remains as are claimed to be representative of the race that made the hand-axe culture, let us briefly consider if there is any evidence which will show us what sort of human type we might expect to find.

In examining the fauna which is associated with the hand-axe culture, two important facts emerged. We found that many species of animals, which in other parts of the world had disappeared from the face of the earth before the Pleistocene period, had continued to live in Africa for a long time and that many of them did not become extinct until the end of the Middle Pleistocene. We also found that there was abundant evidence that *many of the species which are still living in Africa to-day* were already present in a fully evolved form in Middle Pleistocene times, and even a few which show no evolutionary change since the beginning of the Pleistocene. In other words, in many species there is no evidence that since the Middle Pleistocene period any marked evolutionary changes have occurred, and the chief thing that can be said about the Pleistocene period is that it has witnessed the decay and extinction of many earlier types, rather than the birth of new ones. This is in accordance with the evidence from other parts of the world, and there is very little reason to think that, apart from certain domestic animals, any really new animals have been evolved since the beginning of the Middle Pleistocene period, the whole of which, *geologically speaking*, has only occupied a very brief period of time.

If this is true, then upon theoretical evidence we may conclude that man as we know him to-day, man of the species *Homo sapiens*, was probably also fully evolved *physically* by the beginning of the Middle Pleistocene period, unless man has been the one great exception to the general rule of evolution.

We know, of course, that in different parts of the world, in deposits which belong to the Lower and Middle Pleistocene periods, fossil remains have been found which do not represent the species *Homo sapiens* or even the genus Homo. Among such fossils are the famous skulls from Choukoutien near Peking, the Piltdown skull from Sussex, and the skull from Trinil, in Java. We also know that even during the later stages of the Pleistocene a human type which is quite distinct from *Homo sapiens* was still living in southern Europe and in Palestine, a human type known to science as *Homo Neanderthalensis*. Nothing in any of these discoveries of non-*Homo sapiens* types, which were present at different stages of the Pleistocene period but which have now become extinct, is in the least at variance with what we know about other types of mammals, nor does it in the least invalidate the theoretical belief that the species *Homo sapiens* was probably evolved during the early part of the Pleistocene period, and that by Middle Pleistocene times, at latest, his physical evolution as a species was complete. The break-up of a species into geographical races or sub-species is, of course, a quite different thing, and has been going on all through Pleistocene times and is, in fact, still in process.

If we accept as a theory the probability that the species *Homo sapiens* was fully evolved by the Middle Pleistocene period we have to ask ourselves with what culture he was associated. We know that during the Middle Pleistocene there were two distinct major culture complexes. One of these was that which we have called the Chelleo-Acheulean hand-axe culture, and the other the Clactonian-Levalloisian complex, which subsequently gave rise to the Mousterian and developed Levalloisian. Now we know from discoveries in Europe and Palestine that the makers of the developed Levalloisian and Mousterian cultures—which were derived from the Clactonian-Levalloisian culture complex—were men of the Neanderthal species. This being so, if we believe theoretically that the species *Homo sapiens* was in existence in Middle Pleistocene times, we are forced to the conclusion that *in all probability* men of the species *Homo sapiens* were responsible for the great hand-axe culture.

There is another line of argument that also very strongly suggests that the species *Homo sapiens* must have been fully evolved at least in Middle Pleistocene times. In deposits which we know to be of Upper Pleistocene age human remains of various races of *Homo sapiens* have been found in very many parts of the world, from Australia to England and from South Africa to Central Europe. In order to account for such a wide distribution of the species during the later part of the Pleistocene, and for the great amount of subdivision into distinct racial variants of the species, it is absolutely necessary to postulate that the species itself had become fully evolved at a considerably earlier period.

I have discussed at some length the theoretical aspects of the probability (I might almost say, theoretical certainty)[1] that *Homo sapiens* was fully evolved by Middle Pleistocene times, because there are still a great number of people who are so strongly imbued with the old idea that *Homo sapiens* is a *new* and recent evolution—a view that has no theoretical justification whatever—that they think of any reported discovery of remains of *Homo sapiens* in Middle Pleistocene deposits as 'startling' and 'revolutionary', and are consequently greatly prejudiced against its acceptance.

In 1932 the East African Archaeological Expedition discovered some fragments of skulls of *Homo sapiens* type in old lake beds which contain fossil animal remains which are typical of the Middle Pleistocene of Africa, and in the same deposits were found a few hand-axes of the great Chelleo-Acheulean culture. To me, as leader of that Expedition, the evidence is quite clear. These fragments of *Homo sapiens* skull represent men of that species who were living in Middle Pleistocene times. Professor Boswell and others, however, are not yet satisfied as to the age and associations of these discoveries, and in consequence they place the Kanjera human finds in what they term 'the suspense account'. As the whole evidence will probably be rediscussed soon at a conference, I do not propose to say more about a matter that is *sub judice*, but if

---

[1] If the theory of evolution is true, it is *impossible* to explain the wide distribution of races of *Homo sapiens* in Upper Pleistocene times without postulating the existence of the species *Homo sapiens* in Middle Pleistocene times.

the findings of that conference are available in time they
will be given in an appendix to this book.

The question of the age of the small fragment of human
mandible found at Kanam in 1932 is also at present *sub
judice*, but I, personally, am entirely satisfied that it represents the type of man who was living in East Africa during
Lower Pleistocene times and that it represents a form
ancestral to *Homo sapiens*.

In South Africa some confirmation of the association
of man of *Homo sapiens* type with the hand-axe culture
has been found, but I am not aware that any detailed
evidence has yet been made available to the world.

Professor Dreyer, in a letter to *Nature* in April 1935,
states that he has found fragments of a human skull,
which represent the same type of man as my Kanjera
man, in association with the Upper Stellenbosch culture.
He says *inter alia*: 'Here then, we have perfect harmony
between South and East Africa except that Leakey, dealing
with massive deposits from large volumes of water, may
perhaps be overestimating the age of those deposits.'
Professor Dreyer, arguing in a manner which is most
unconvincing to any one with geological knowledge, holds
that the Upper Stellenbosch culture in South Africa
belongs to a period only just before 'Recent' times. The
evidence that has been put forward in Chapter V, however,
shows that the view does not fit in with the available
geological and faunal evidence, which suggests that the
Upper Stellenbosch culture of South Africa belongs rather
to the closing stages of the Middle Pleistocene.

In addition to the reported discovery of a fragmentary
human skull with a late stage of the hand-axe culture,
South Africa has provided us with a number of other
discoveries of remains of the men of different periods of
the Stone Age.

Unfortunately, not all of these finds are well documented. In 1913 parts of a human skull, including most of the top of the skull and a fragment of the jaw, were found at Boskop in the Transvaal during the cutting of a drainage trench on the farm of a Mr. Botha. The Boskop skull was associated with some flakes which, at the time, were regarded as of 'crude Mousterian workmanship'. The skull is that of a very large man, and Sir Arthur Keith has pointed out that its affinities are with the skulls of Bushmen and also with the skulls of 'the Strand-loopers' who were responsible for the shell-mounds of South Africa at the end of the Stone Age.

The evidence seems to suggest that the Boskop man was the maker of one of the many cultural variations which are included in the 'Middle Stone Age complex' of South Africa, but such an association is not absolutely proved.

At Tzitzikama, on the coast of South Africa about 100 miles west of Port Elizabeth, Mr. Fitzsimons discovered in 1921 a series of cave-deposits which contained human remains as well as stone implements. The skulls found here represent the same racial type as the Boskop man, and the culture, so far as I can determine it on the basis of the illustrated material, belongs to one of the variations of the 'Middle Stone Age complex', thus confirming the evidence which the Boskop find suggested to us.

Another important find of human remains associated with tools which belong to one of the many variations of the 'Middle Stone Age complex' is the skull and partial skeleton from the Springbok Flats not far from Pretoria. I had the privilege of examining this skull for a short time at Pretoria Museum in 1929, and it seemed to me to resemble closely some of the skulls which in East Africa are associated with the Elmenteitan culture.

Although there were no implements found in direct contact with the Springbok Flats skull many implements were nearby, and there is little doubt that the implements and the human bones are of approximately the same date. This view is strengthened by the fact that bones of the giant extinct buffalo, *Bubalus bainei*, were found with the human bones, and this animal is known to have been contemporary with the 'Middle Stone Age culture complex'.

Early in 1929 Professor Drennan was fortunate enough to discover some human skull fragments at a sand-pit at Cape Flats. These fragments were not found *in situ* but had been brought to light by those who were engaged in exploiting the sand-pit for commercial purposes. In spite of the absence of direct evidence, the condition of the bones, the colour which they were stained, and the adhering soil are regarded by him as pointing to the fact that they had been derived from the lower deposits exposed in the wall of the pit and not from the top modern sands.

One of the two skulls from this site resembles in many ways that from Springbok Flats and, like the latter, recalls some of the skulls found with the Elmenteitan culture in Kenya. The other skull apparently represented a modern type of Bushman. According to some of the reports the implements found at this site were of two distinct types, some of them recalling the culture found in the late shell-mounds and others recalling one of the 'Middle Stone Age cultures'. This Cape Flats skull is regarded by South African anatomists as representing what they call the 'Australoid' prehistoric race of South Africa, and Professor Broom believes that even in certain living South African tribes he can detect 'Australoid' characteristics, but I do not think the description is a good one.

Another skull which is attributed to one of the 'Middle Stone Age cultures' is the Fishhoek skull, which is said to be definitely associated with the Stillbay culture. This skull was found by Mr. Peers during the excavation of a rock-shelter, which yielded a series of occupational levels with different Stone Age cultures.

If the attribution of the Fishhoek skull to the Stillbay culture is correct, it is very interesting indeed, and I see no reason for doubting the evidence for the excavations were carried out very carefully, and the skull was found *in situ*.

The Fishhoek skull, which is quite complete, has many very close resemblances to the skulls of modern Bushmen, but is bigger and more robust, and represents just such a stage through which we should expect the Bushman races to have passed. We have already seen in the last chapter that the modern Bushmen of a few hundred years ago were artists, and also we have seen that the evidence of the Bambata Cave in Southern Rhodesia points to the fact that the earlier paintings were the work of a race who had a culture very closely resembling the Stillbay culture. The Fishhoek skull, therefore, adds a link to the chain of evidence and suggests that, of the various prehistoric South African races, it was those of the Bushman stock who were responsible for much of the art.

In addition to the skulls mentioned above from South Africa, there are a good many others concerning which I have, unfortunately, no data. Most of them, however, so far as can be judged from references, have been found in association with the very late Stone Age cultures, such as the Wilton and the shell-mound cultures.

Farther north in Northern Rhodesia we come to the site of the most-discussed prehistoric skull yet found in Africa, the Broken Hill skull.

It is exceedingly unfortunate that there is so little

accurate evidence available in connexion with this skull, for, unlike any other skulls found so far in the African continent, it does not belong to the species *Homo sapiens*, but is more closely related to the Neanderthal stock found in Europe, although it is different in certain important characters.

The Broken Hill skull was found in 1921 by a Swiss workman called Zwiglar during the course of mining operations at the mine after which the skull is named. The hill, or kopje, where the mining operations were being carried out, had in it a great cave which was filled up with vast quantities of broken bones and stone implements. These cave-deposits had become completely impregnated with zinc and lead salts, and, in consequence, the deposits were being treated as ore and smelted.

Mining had been in process for very many years and, as long as fourteen years before the discovery of the skull was reported, a geologist, Mr. F. P. Mennel, who had visited the mine in connexion with his professional duties, had called attention to the fact that these cave-deposits at Broken Hill were full of Stone Age man's implements. He recorded that there were at least four distinct occupational levels of the site and that the deposits had 'accumulated during alternate occupations of the original cave by animals and human beings, with intervening periods when the cave was untenanted owing probably to flooding with water'.[1]

From 1907 to 1921 no further news of the Broken Hill cave reached the world, although mining operations continued, and when Zwiglar made his great discovery the work had reached a low level, and it was not in the upper but in the lower part of the deposits that the skull was

[1] 'An African occurrence of Fossil Mammalia associated with Stone implements', *Geol.*, May 1907, p. 443, by F. P. Mennel.

found. It is quite certain that there were many animal bones found at the same level as the skull, and we can presume that stone implements were also present, but none of these were recovered. It was unfortunate that, while the upper part of the cave deposits was impregnated with zinc, the lower part was chiefly impregnated with lead. As a result the material dug from the upper deposits was, for the time being, placed in enormous dumps not far from the mine (these dumps had still not been touched in 1929 when I visited the site), while the lower deposits with their lead salts were put straight into trucks and taken to be smelted, for at that time it was chiefly the lead from Broken Hill mine which was being worked, and the zinc ores were being dumped for future work.

Although a good many fossil animal bones were sent to England with the skull, and although these were reported to have been associated with the skull, evidence collected by Dr. Hrdlicka and others tends to show that these animal remains come from the upper deposits, while the skull was from lower down.

The fossil animal bones which were sent to England for examination represented, almost entirely, species which are still living to-day, but there is no positive evidence to show whether the fauna actually found with the skull (and subsequently smelted for its lead content) was also mainly composed of living species, or whether it had many extinct forms.

Although we have, therefore, to face the fact that the age of the Broken Hill skull is uncertain, it is of very great interest because of its resemblances and relationship to the Neanderthal species of Europe and western Asia. We know that in Europe the Neanderthal species is associated with the group of cultures which includes the Mousterian and the Levalloisian, and we know that in Africa cultures which can be referred to this group on typological grounds are present, and it is more than likely that men of the type represented by the Broken Hill skull were the makers of the earlier Levalloisian types of culture in Africa. Sooner or later another site like the Broken Hill cave is sure to be found, and the evidence which was lost at that site will become available once more.

Going northwards from Rhodesia we come again to East Africa, which, as we saw at the beginning of this chapter, has yielded some fragmentary human remains, for which I claim an early date but which are at present *sub judice*. In addition to these controversial finds, human remains have been found at a number of other sites in association with the later stages of the Stone Age of East Africa.[1]

At Gamble's Cave at Elmenteita parts of five skulls and skeletons were found in association with phase *c* of the Upper Kenya Aurignacian. Two of these were in a reasonably complete condition. They were tall, heavily built individuals, with large skulls and straight faces instead of the prognathous faces of typical negroes, and in other characters, too, they can be regarded as 'non-negroid' although there are some features, such as the shape of the forehead, in which these skulls resemble the negro rather than any other racial type.

These makers of the last stage of the Aurignacian culture in Kenya were buried in an ultra-contracted position in the rock-shelter in which they lived, and their bodies were covered in red ochre before being buried, suggesting that the colour red had some ceremonial significance.

In 1913 Professor Reck had discovered a human skeleton at Oldoway, which had also been buried in the

---

[1] For a detailed account of the East African human remains see *The Stone Age Races of Kenya*, 1935, L. S. B. Leakey.

contracted position. This Oldoway skeleton was at first thought to be *in situ* in Bed II at Oldoway, and to come from a horizon which has since yielded Chellean types of implement. The skeleton lay in deposits of Bed II and was overlain by a layer of red material which was thought to represent undisturbed Bed III. Subsequent work has shown that this overlying red material was *not* undisturbed Bed III, but was a mixture of Bed III deposits with other later deposits, and evidence was obtained that the Oldoway man was really the contemporary of a late stage of the Aurignacian culture, and that he had been *buried into Bed II* and then covered over with red material of Bed III mixed with later deposits. The red material which covered the burial site of the Oldoway skeleton may have been formed by natural agencies in the form of a hill-wash, or possibly it represents material brought by the men of the period and put over the burial for ceremonial purposes in the same way that the Aurignacian skeletons at Gamble's Cave were covered with red ochre.

The Oldoway skull is of the same physical type as the Gamble's Cave skulls and represents a race that was not negro[1] but had *some* negroid affinities.

Associated with the Elmenteitan culture of East Africa, over twenty human skulls have been found. They represent a decidedly mixed race in which some individuals have a close resemblance to the makers of the late Kenya Aurignacian culture, while others are much more like the human type which in South Africa is represented by the Springbok Flats skull. While most of these makers of the Elmenteitan

---

[1] When we say that a race which is represented by fossil skulls was not negro, we do not necessarily mean that the skin colour was not dark. We cannot tell. What we mean is that the skulls are not of the form which is typical of true negroes to-day. It must also be remembered that there are dark-skinned races in Africa even to-day that have non-negro skulls in this sense.

culture were tall and strongly built, a few were very short and hardly larger than present-day pygmies.

Unfortunately, we have not yet found any skulls in East Africa in association with either the Levalloisian or the Stillbay culture, although we have three teeth representing the makers of the latter.[1]

The makers of the earlier stages of the Wilton culture in Kenya, as well as of the Magosian, are as yet unknown, but we have a number of skulls and skeletons of the men who were responsible for the shell-mounds, which, as we have seen, yield a late form of the Wilton culture of East Africa. These shell-mound people in East Africa closely resemble the shell-mound people of some of the South African sites, and were probably of the same stock. Although they were tall, strongly built people with very big heads, and big brains, they have distinct affinities with the Bushmen.

In contrast to these makers of the Wilton culture of the shell-mounds with their Bushman affinities, the makers of the Neolithic cultures which we call Gumban were of a physical type which is almost European. They were tall, well-built people with big brains, and their faces, and in particular their noses, were of European type. What their skin colour was we cannot, of course, tell. The makers of the Gumban A culture were in the habit of removing the central incisors of the lower jaw, much in the way that some African tribes do to-day, while the makers of the Gumban B culture did not have this practice.

The Gumban A race buried their dead in shallow holes in the ground, and the site was then marked by a small cairn of stones.

[1] In the *East African Standard* of Feb. 1936, the discovery of human remains with a Levalloisian culture is reported from Karungu in Kenya, but confirmatory information is at present lacking.

The Gumban B race, on the other hand, buried their dead up against a small cliff or slope and then built a very large cairn over the burial. Both races placed the body in the ultra-contracted position.

Of the makers of the Njoroan Neolithic culture and the Tumbian we, as yet, know nothing.

From East Africa we turn to the North, and in French North Africa we find that the makers of the Capsian and the Oranian (i.e. Ibero-Maurusian) cultures are comparatively well known.

The best material representing the makers of the Capsian culture is that from Metcha-el-Arbi, while a magnificent series of skulls representing the makers of the Oranian (I-M) culture has been recently described from cave excavations at Beni Segoual.[1] It seems as though the makers of these two cultures (which have a different regional distribution) were of the same racial type, and that they must be regarded simply as different tribes of a single race.

In this connexion Vaufrey says, in his summary of the relationship between the Capsian and the Oranian cultures: 'Il convient de se rappeler que si Capsiens et Ibéro-maurusians eurent des industries de facies profondément divergents, ils n'en appartenaient pas moins à une seule et même race, celle de Metcha el Arbi.' With this view Professors Boule and Vallois concur in their account of the skulls from Beni Segoual.

In comparing this North African with other Stone Age races from other parts of the world, the closest parallels are found with the so-called Cromagnon race, which was responsible for the later stages of the Aurignacian culture in Europe. At the same time it is clear that, from a study

[1] *Archives de l'Institut de Paléontologie Humaine*, Mémoire No. 13, Paris, 1934.

of the North African material, there had already been some degree of racial mixing, for certain individuals skulls in the series are not really typical of the Cromagnon race.

It is interesting, too, to note that whereas in Europe none of the skulls belonging to the Cromagnon race show any trace of deliberate dental mutilation, the skulls found with the Capsian and Oranian (I-M) cultures almost invariably have the central incisors of the upper jaw (and very occasionally of the lower jaw also) missing, and examination shows that the teeth were extracted at an early age. This custom of teeth extraction has already been noticed in some of the Neolithic skulls of East Africa, and its occurrence in the late Upper Palaeolithic skulls is of especial interest in view of the fact that the custom is still widespread in Africa to-day.

Some early writers have suggested that the North African skulls of the Metcha-el-Arbi type show resemblances to those of the Neanderthal species, but this view is not confirmed by the latest investigations of Professors Boule and Vallois. On the other hand, although the chief resemblances are with the Cromagnon race, certain characters also recall some of the Elmenteitan skulls and the so-called 'Australoid' type in South Africa.

Although a number of sites in North Africa have yielded implements belonging to the Levalloisian culture and its derivative, the Aterian, no associated human remains have as yet been found, and the same is unfortunately true as far as the Chelleo-Acheulean culture is concerned. On the other hand, there are a number of finds in French North Africa which can be attributed to the later Neolithic cultures, but I have not been able to obtain any accurate data concerning them.

Finally, in French North Africa, we have to mention

PLATE XI

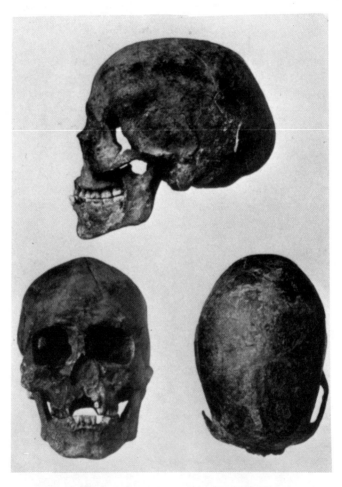

The fossil skull from Asselar (male)
(From *Archives de l'Institut de Paléontologie Humaine*,
Mémoire No. 9, by permission of Professor M. Boule)

PLATE XII

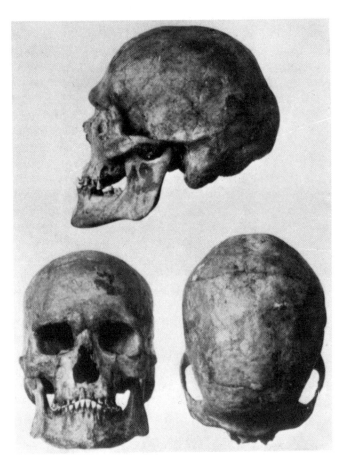

The fossil skull No. 12 from Beni Segoual (male)
(From *Archives de l'Institut de Paléontologie Humaine*,
Mémoire No. 13, by permission of Professor M. Boule)

PLATE XIII

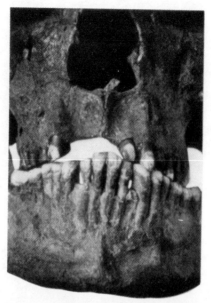

a

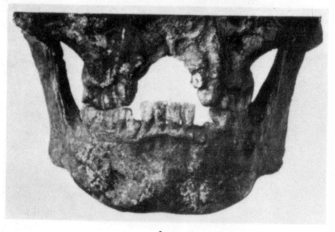

b

Views of the dentition of (*a*) a skull from Beni Segoual,
(*b*) the Asselar skull, to illustrate the dental mutilation
(From *Archives de l'Institut de Paléontologie Humaine*, Mémoires
No. 9 and 13, by permission of Professor M. Boule)

the fossil skull and skeleton which was found at Asselar, about 220 miles north-east of Timbuctoo.

Unfortunately, no stone implements were found with this Asselar skeleton, but the circumstances under which it was found show that it belongs to a prehistoric and not a recent period.

At Asselar, which is to-day in the desert, the deposits in which the skeleton lay were found to be lake deposits in which fossil remains of fish, crocodiles, and mollusca occurred. The authors of the publication in which the Asselar skull is described consider that this evidence points to an Upper Pleistocene date, and with this view I agree. From the detailed study which they have made, Professors Boule and Vallois have come to the conclusion that the Asselar skull, unlike the skulls associated with the Capsian and Oranian cultures and unlike the Stone Age skulls from East Africa, has very marked negro or negroid characters. This is very interesting for, if the dating given is accepted, we are thus provided with a true representative of the Stone Age ancestors of the negro stock of Central Africa.

In the eastern part of the North African region, that is to say the Nile Valley, the only human fragments which represent the makers of any of the Upper Pleistocene cultures are some skull fragments which are associated with the early stages of the Sebilian culture at Kom Ombo, together with some fragments from Kau, which are assumed by Dr. Sandford to be of that age for a variety of reasons. The Kau finds were associated with fossilized remains of animals which included some extinct species.

Sandford states that the preliminary reports (as yet unpublished as far as I know) on these human skull fragments 'are more akin to the Predynastic Egyptian than to any other race of which we have full knowledge', and

N

he adds: 'The recognition of the Predynastic type at a date by the balance of probabilities, Palaeolithic, is an important event and one from which other discoveries will probably arise.'

Associated with some of the Neolithic and Predynastic cultures of Egypt, a considerable number of human remains have been found, while as yet we have no knowledge of the makers of other Neolithic cultures such as that from the Fayum. Except in minor details, most of the Neolithic races of Egypt do not appear to differ very greatly from the Egyptians of the Dynastic period. As it would be quite beyond the scope of this chapter, I will not attempt to discuss these Egyptian Neolithic races here.

One of the most noteworthy facts that emerges from our summary of the Stone Age races of Africa is that in the Upper Pleistocene period there were already present in Africa a number of distinct and well-differentiated races of the species *Homo sapiens*. In South Africa there were at least two races, one of which was ancestral to the Bushmen and Hottentots of modern times, and the other representing a non-negroid race related to the non-negroid races which were present in East Africa at the same time. Among present-day races these early non-negroids stand nearest to some of the tribes which are commonly spoken of as Hamitic, and in consequence they may perhaps be regarded as a proto-Hamitic strain which at a later date mixed with a negroid strain, and so gave rise to the African Hamitic peoples of the present day.

The great stronghold of the true negro type to-day is the Congo and West Africa, and we have seen that at Asselar in the southern Sahara region there is evidence that the negro type was already developed in Upper Pleistocene times. In Egypt, on the evidence from Kom Ombo and Kau, the racial type which gave rise to the predynastic races and to the Egyptians was also already differentiated, while in French North Africa there was a race which, though distinct, had affinities with the Cromagnon race of Europe as well as with the proto-Hamitic races of East and South Africa. This evidence—even if we leave out of account the various races of *Homo sapiens* that were in other parts of the world in the Upper Pleistocene period[1]—leads to only one possible conclusion, and that is that the species *Homo sapiens* must have been in existence in a fully evolved form in the Middle Pleistocene period. If we are right, and if the makers of the great Chelleo-Acheulean hand-axe culture were men of this species, then the very wide geographical distribution of that culture suggests further that even in Middle Pleistocene times there were probably several quite distinct races of the species *Homo sapiens* in existence. Time and further well conducted discoveries will alone prove whether this was so.

[1] In China, in Australia, in Russia, in France, in England, &c., *Homo sapiens* skulls which are dated as Upper Pleistocene have been found.

CHAPTER X

THE STONE AGE IN AFRICA
COMPARED WITH EUROPE

IN Africa we have seen that the available evidence from
regions as far apart as North and South Africa presents
us with a picture that is remarkably similar except in
points of detail. In East and South Africa there is evidence
that during Lower Pleistocene times early races of men
who made crude implements of pebble type were living
side by side with animals of archaic type, many of which
have long since become extinct, although there were also
present some species which have survived up to the present
day practically unchanged. In North Africa, although the
fauna of the Lower Pleistocene, as far as it is known, compares well with that of East and South Africa at the same
time, there is as yet no evidence of an early pre-Chellean
cultural stage. We cannot say whether such a culture
never existed there, or whether it has merely not yet been
found.

In Europe at about the same time there is evidence that
one or more very primitive pre-Chellean cultures were
present, and of these the Darmsdenian is a pebble culture
which may have affinities with the earliest Kafuan of East
Africa.

In Africa we find that at the beginning of the Middle
Pleistocene period the early stages of the great hand-axe
culture, the Chelleo-Acheulean, come on the scene, and
throughout the Middle Pleistocene the gradually develop-
ing stages of this culture hold a dominant place. In south-
western Europe, too, this is the case,[1] and various stages

[1] In making this statement I am adhering to my definition of the
term Pleistocene. According to some other definitions the deposits

of the great hand-axe culture are typical of the Middle Pleistocene period. Neither in Africa nor yet in south-western Europe is the Chelleo-Acheulean culture the only one that is represented in deposits of the Middle Pleistocene. In both areas we find that there are also assemblages of stone implements which have to be assigned to one or other of the different branches of the great Levalloisian-Clactonian-Mousterian group of cultures.

Not only is this the case, but in both continents we find that wherever this overlapping of these two great culture complexes has taken place, there is some evidence that they have affected each other, and that the contact of cultures has given birth to cultural hybrids to which we often have to give new and special distinguishing names.

In Africa, cultures such as the Sangoan, the Nanyukian, the Pseudo-Stillbay, the Fauresmith, and that branch of the Upper Stellenbosch culture which is characterized by cores of the Victoria West type, are some of the cultural hybrids which probably owe their origin to the over-lapping of the two great earlier culture complexes.

In south-west Europe, cultures such as the Micoquian and the Upper Levalloisian cultural stages in which hand axes are present are also probably the result of the over-lap, and the extraordinary similarity between some of the hybrid cultures in Europe and in Africa gives us one of our earliest examples of how cultural similarities can be developed independently from common ancestral forms, or, in other words, illustrates for us the processes of parallel evolution.

When we consider the distribution of the great Chelleo-

---

in which the earliest stages of the Chellean culture appear in Europe are regarded as Lower Pleistocene, but according to these the deposits which we call Middle Pleistocene in Africa would also have to be called Lower Pleistocene.

Acheulean culture and the extraordinary similarity of the type tools of the different stages of that culture in south-west Europe and all over Africa, we are forced to ask ourselves whether this similarity is due to a series of successive waves of migration from some central point where the process of hand-axe evolution was going on, or whether migrations only occurred occasionally, and parallel evolution was responsible for the other similarities.

In Africa the artefacts of the Chellean stages of the great hand-axe culture do not include true cleavers, but in the Acheulean stages cleavers of several very distinct types become common and typical. In south-west Europe cleavers are also absent in the earlier stages of the hand-axe culture, but occur (although much less commonly) in the later stages of the Acheulean.

Is the appearance of the cleaver in the Acheulean of Europe to be explained on the grounds of a fresh migration from Africa by a branch of the race that made the hand-axe culture in Africa, or did the cleaver evolve independently in South, East, and North Africa and in Europe?

In Europe certain stages of the Acheulean culture are marked by the presence of ovate-shaped hand-axes which, when looked at edge-on, show a most remarkable curved cutting edge which is commonly called an 'S twist'. Identical 'S twist' ovates occur in certain stages of the Acheulean in East Africa and elsewhere. Is this to be attributed to migrations or to parallel evolution?

In other words, once the earliest stages of the hand-axe culture had spread far and wide over Africa and south-west Europe (not to mention a part of Asia), did the makers of the early and crude hand-axes of each area gradually evolve and develop new forms for themselves, or were new forms evolved one in one area and one in another, and were these new forms then spread to the other areas by migratory movements?

As far as Europe is concerned it certainly looks as though there is no positive evidence for a direct local evolution from the Chellean to the Acheulean stages, and it seems rather that a cold glacial period either exterminated or drove southwards to Africa the makers of the Chellean culture, and that when the climate once more became suitable, men who had reached an Acheulean stage of culture in North Africa, a stage in which cleavers had already been evolved, re-invaded South-west Europe taking this more developed stage of the hand-axe culture with them.

If this is the true explanation, then what are we to say about the different regions of the great African continent? Is local parallel evolution from a cruder and earlier form of the hand-axe culture to be held to account for the amazing similarity between the assemblages of tools which represent the later stages of the hand-axe culture in South, East, and North Africa? I think not. I think that, without the necessity of postulating mass migrations, we can assume that new ideas, once evolved, were rapidly passed on from one area to another. And yet the evidence that in many areas the effects of a contact between the Chelleo-Acheulean culture and the Levalloisian-Clactonian complex led to parallel evolution of hybrid cultures, stands as a warning to us, and the possibility that highly specialized tools such as cleavers and 'S twist' ovates may have evolved in different areas as a result of parallel evolution cannot be entirely neglected.

The suggestion made above that, at any rate as far as south-west Europe is concerned, we should attribute the presence of cleavers in the Acheulean stages of culture to a re-invasion of a hand-axe-making people from North

Africa when climatic conditions improved once again after a glacial period, raises at once the question as to whether there were land-bridges linking South-west Europe and North Africa across the Mediterranean at the time.

As we saw in Chapter I, Vaufrey and some other recent students of this problem hold that positive evidence for such land-bridges in the Pleistocene is wanting, and particularly as far as the hypothetical Italy–Sicily–Malta–Tunis bridge is concerned.

Among the arguments adduced is the latest evidence of the depths of the channels which separate these land masses, and it is pointed out that the known changes of land- and sea-level in the Mediterranean area would not have been sufficient to transform these channels into land-bridges.

So far as a land-bridge during the last stages of the Pleistocene is concerned, this argument holds good, and the faunal evidence given in Chapter II supports it. But in Chapter I we saw that there is now abundant evidence that at the end of the Middle Pleistocene *and after the final stages of the Acheulean culture had evolved*, there were very great movements of the earth's crust accompanied by faulting, tilting, and by folding. Nor were these movements confined to the Rift Valley zone, for in North Africa deposits containing an Acheulean cultural stage have been shown to have been affected.

My own view is that at least during a part of the Lower and Middle Pleistocene period there was probably a land-bridge linking North Africa with South-west Europe, and that the breaking of this bridge was not so much due to changes in land- and sea-level as to earthquakes and earth movements and faults at the time of the last great faulting in the Rift Valley zone. The absence of the Chelleo-Acheulean culture in Sicily and South Italy and its presence in Spain suggests that possibly the land-bridge was in the Gibraltar region and not between Sicily and Tunis.[1]

Up to the closing stages of the Middle Pleistocene period we have seen that the Stone Age cultures which were present in South, East, and North Africa and in South-western Europe were very similar indeed, but at the period which marks the end of the Middle Pleistocene and the beginning of the Upper Pleistocene this marked similarity becomes much less pronounced.

In North Africa, during the period which follows upon that occupied by the later stages of the great hand-axe culture, we find that (so far as available evidence shows) for a time the Levalloisian-Mousterian culture was the only culture present, while in East Africa it was coexistent with a very crude and early stage of a typical Aurignacian culture of the African type as distinct from what is known as the Asiatic Aurignacian.[2]

Such evidence as is available suggests that the early Aurignacian development in Kenya was itself one of the consequences of the culture contact of which we have already spoken. This view that an Acheuleo-Levalloisian contact may give rise to a form of Aurignacian is supported by discoveries made in the south of France by M. Péyrony who has described what he calls a 'Moustérien à tradition Acheuléan', in which the effect of the contact is the evolution of certain tools which are the prototypes of the typical

[1] We need a great deal more evidence about the fauna associated with the hand-axe culture in the soūth of Spain, for it is possible that man alone was able to move between Africa and Europe at this time, either by swimming or on rafts.

[2] The African Aurignacian is characterized by the presence of many 'backed blades', angle burins, end-scrapers, and some lunates and other microlithic tools, while the Asiatic Aurignacian is characterized by keeled scrapers, burins of a different type, and the very rare occurrence of backed blades.

burins and backed blades of the Lower Aurignacian of Europe.

Here, then, we are again apparently faced with a parallel evolution in two widely separated areas.

In East Africa this culture contact apparently gave rise to several other hybrid cultures in addition to the early Aurignacian, and of these the Nanyukian is closely paralleled by the Fauresmith culture of South Africa. In East Africa, however, the Nanyukian only lasted for a very short time, but in South Africa the Fauresmith culture flourished and passed through a number of evolutionary stages.

The North African evidence suggests that the Capsian and Oranian cultures arrived fully developed and rather late in the Upper Pleistocene. This fact, together with the close similarity between the earliest Capsian and the later and more developed stages of the East African Aurignacian, is favourable to the view that the Capsian and Oranian arrived in North Africa from the East African region.

There is, as we have seen, no longer any reason to believe that the Capsian of North Africa was the source of origin of the Lower Aurignacian of Europe, for, on the one hand, the earliest Capsian in North Africa is much more developed than the earliest Aurignacian of Europe, and on the other, there is suggestive evidence from France that the earliest European Aurignacian was a purely local development along parallel lines to those which gave rise to the African Aurignacian in Kenya.

If there was at any time a movement of the Capsian culture across the Mediterranean into south Europe, it was probably at the very end of the Pleistocene period, and *latest* Upper Aurignacian culture stages in Spain and the south of France seem to have elements which are possibly derived from North Africa.

After evolving in East Africa it seems as though the African Aurignacian culture spread north-east and north-west, for it is found both in North Africa and in Somaliland, but it never seems to have penetrated very far southwards in a pure form. Its influence was, however, felt, and possibly stray bands of men belonging to the race which made it went southwards, for, as we have seen, the Bambata culture and the Stillbay and the Mazeppa culture all seem to reflect an Aurignacian influence.

And at this point we again come face to face with the question as to how much we can attribute to parallel evolution and how much to direct spreads of culture. In East Africa, after existing side by side for some time, the Aurignacian culture and the developed Levalloisian affected each other in such a way as to give rise to what we call the East African Stillbay culture, which, in addition to having elements derived from both the Aurignacian and Levalloisian, has also certain new types of artefact which are sometimes leaf-shaped, sometimes triangular, and sometimes lozenge-shaped, but which are usually delicately worked by a pressure-flaking technique over at least a part of both surfaces.

The Bambata culture and the Stillbay culture of South Africa are characterized by a similar admixture of elements from both the Levalloisian and Aurignacian cultures, and, in addition, they too have these special pressure-flaked artefacts. Did this curious hybrid culture spread from one single point at which it was evolved, or did the East African Stillbay, the South-African Stillbay, and the Rhodesian Stillbay (i.e. Bambata culture) each develop independently but along identical lines as a result of having similar parentage?

I am strongly inclined to believe that in this instance we are definitely dealing with cases of parallel evolution

and not of diffusion, for when we turn to North Africa
we find that the developed Levalloisian of that region—
apparently as a result of contact with or influences from
the African Aurignacian culture which was spreading
northward—evolved into what is known as the Aterian
culture, which is by no means identical with the various
Stillbay groups, but which nevertheless has pressure-
flaked, leaf-shaped, and lozenge-shaped tools in common
with them.

In Europe, too, we find that something of a similar
nature happened. In many ways the Solutrean culture
very closely resembles the Stillbay of South and East
Africa and the Aterian of North Africa, except that the
Levalloisian elements are very much less noticeable
(except perhaps in the Proto-Solutrean of Central Europe).
Like the Stillbay culture, however, the Solutrean has
Aurignacian elements in addition to leaf-shaped tools
made by a pressure-flaking technique.

Still more interesting, perhaps, from the point of view
of parallel evolution is the fact that it is almost certain
that the Aurignacian elements in the Solutrean are derived
from the Asiatic Aurignacian which was apparently
spreading into West Europe from Asia, while the Aurignacian elements in the Stillbay and Aterian cultures are
of different origin.

There are some ardent diffusionists who will probably
consider that any suggestions of similarities being due to
parallel evolution and not to the spread of culture influences are unwarrantable, but I cannot see that it is in any
way possible to account for the resemblances between
the Solutrean, the Aterian, and the Stillbay cultures
except on the 'parallel evolution' basis.

As far as the various subdivisions of the Stillbay culture
are concerned and also perhaps the Aterian, *it is possible*

that the true explanation is to be found in the diffusionist theory, but, as I have said, I do not think so.

At this stage, we must turn for a moment to a consideration of whether the prehistoric art of Europe and of different parts of Africa will throw any light upon the conflict between the principles of independent evolution and diffusion.

The prehistoric art of South-west Europe, and particularly the art of Eastern Spain, has been frequently compared with some of the South African Stone Age art, and the discoveries of cave paintings in East Africa and in North Africa have been held to be the links between the Eastern Spanish and the South African art.

In 1929 Burkitt wrote:[1]

'. . . it may be noted that a cave with paintings in a somewhat similar style has lately been discovered in this latter area [the Southern Sahara]. . . . This discovery in turn connects the art of our area [South Africa] with that of East Spain where the paintings at Cogul . . . &c. very closely resemble the ''Bushman'' art or to be more accurate the earlier series of paintings found in Southern Rhodesia.'

In 1931 Professor Breuil, in summarizing his views on the prehistoric cultures and art of Africa, wrote:[2]

'My opinion, then, is that both as far as the paintings and the engravings are concerned, the oldest, which are contemporary with the ''Middle Stone Age'' where the influence of the Upper Palaeolithic is certain, are apparently more or less contemporary with our Upper Palaeolithic, and are truly connected in origin with the art of Eastern Spanish rock-shelters and certain paintings and engravings in the Sahara and Lybia.'

In another passage he says:

'And so both in its art on the walls of caves or on rock slabs,

[1] *South Africa's Past in Stone and Paint*, M. C. Burkitt, 1929.
[2] Translated from his article in *Cahiers d'Art*, Paris, 1931.

and in the sequence of its Stone Age industries, South Africa shows unquestionable relationships with the past of Western Europe, without doubt due to the fact that waves of humanity and of civilizations, starting more or less at the same time from some intermediate point which is as yet not fixed, reached these two extremities of the Old World.'

Since the passages which I have quoted were written, a good many fresh discoveries have been made concerning both the prehistoric art and the cultures in Africa. Vaufrey has put forward evidence that even the earliest development of the Capsian culture in North Africa is later than the Lower Aurignacian of Europe, but he has also shown that the Capsian culture rather than the Oranian (Ibero-Maurusian) has affinities with the Aurignacian culture of Spain, so that the evidence suggesting a link between the Eastern Spanish art and some of the North African art has been *slightly* strengthened.

The discovery of a series of superpositions in the prehistoric art in Tanganyika Territory very strongly suggests that some of it is of considerable age, but it would not be safe on the basis of what we know at present to make any direct comparisons with the art of Southern Rhodesia. Before that can be done excavations must be carried out in order to try to discover the nature of the culture stages of the artists responsible for the different styles.

If some of the earliest East African art proves eventually to be associated with the East African Aurignacian culture, then we will have good reason for believing that these East African Aurignacian people were perhaps the people who spread artistic ideas over Africa. But the IF is a big one. If the earliest art of Tanganyika proves to be associated with the local form of the Stillbay culture in the same way that the earliest art of Southern Rhodesia seems to be associated with the Bambata culture, then we should probably have to regard the art of each area as having evolved independently, for the evidence of excavations at sites such as Apis Rock in East Africa and Bambata in Southern Rhodesia suggests that in each case the Stillbay (or Bambata) culture evolved locally as a result of an Aurignacian-Levalloisian contact.

But in South Africa by no means all the art is associated with the Stillbay culture. Most of the engravings are believed to be the work of the makers of the Smithfield culture, while many of the later paintings are probably due to the makers of the Wilton culture. Most of the available evidence suggests that the Smithfield culture was of local evolution in South Africa,[1] and yet, as we have seen, Breuil considers that some of the earlier engravings in the Sahara are so identical to some in South Africa that he says 'the analogy with South Africa is too strong to be a coincidence'. If this is so, then the links between these two areas of rock engravings have yet to be found.

It seems to me that some of the prehistoric art of Europe, the early Aurignacian and Magdalenian art in particular, has no connexion with the early art of Africa, even if some links between the Eastern Spanish art and that of North Africa are accepted. If this is so, and there is thus evidence of independent artistic developments in these two regions, I cannot see why diffusion should of necessity be called to our aid to account for prehistoric art in different parts of the African continent.

I see no reason to believe that at different times and in different regions men with artistic talents should not have been born and have evolved an art of their own, sometimes naturalistic and sometimes of a conventionalized style.

---

[1] Some people see a link between the Smithfield culture and certain industries found in Egypt, the link being the highly specialized 'concavo-convex side-scraper'.

From this brief discussion of the art, we turn again to the cultures. During the later stages of the Stone Age we find that cultures characterized by very small artefacts, called Microliths, have a very wide distribution in Africa. The various developments of the Wilton culture in South Africa, Rhodesia, and East Africa, the Gumban Neolithic cultures, are all examples of this, as are the later stages of the Sebilian culture, and some of the French North African cultures such as the later Upper Capsian. In Europe the Tardenoisian culture falls into the same category. Some writers consider that all of these Microlithic cultures spread from some one single centre at which they were evolved. Breuil, in his summary of the Stone Age in Africa in *Cahiers d'Art*, says: 'As for the Microlithic cultures, North Africa from Tunis to Egypt seems to be an important centre of diffusion from which branches have spread out afar to Europe, Asia Minor, India perhaps, and right down to the extreme south [of Africa].'

This interpretation does not seem to me to fit the facts. In East Africa the true Aurignacian had *in its later* stage many typical Microlithic artefacts, and from the later stages of the Upper Kenya Aurignacian there developed locally a number of cultures such as the Wilton A and the Gumban Neolithic: cultures which are essentially Microlithic in character.

Also, from the Kenya Aurignacian, but in an indirect way, the Microlithic culture known as Wilton B developed, but in this case the development was through a Stillbay and a Magosian phase.

In Southern Rhodesia it seems to me more reasonable to derive the local form of the Wilton from the equally local form of Magosian which evolved from the Bambata or Stillbay culture. The latter may have been originally due to the impact of Aurignacian influence upon a Levalloisian culture, so that possibly the Wilton of Rhodesia can be ultimately traced back to the same source as the Wilton of Kenya.

In North Africa at Sebil, the Early Sebilian gradually evolves by way of a Middle Sebilian stage into a true Microlithic stage known as the Upper Sebilian. In so far as the Early Sebilian was probably derived from a Levalloisian-Aurignacian contact, the Microlithic phase of the Sebilian can be traced back ultimately to Aurignacian influence. In the western parts of the North African littoral, as we have already seen, the earliest known stage of the Capsian culture has a certain Microlithic element which in the processes of evolution becomes dominant in the 'Neolithic of Capsian tradition'.

In Europe there is equally no need to regard the Microlithic cultures as having spread from some single source after they had been evolved, for in the Upper Palaeolithic cultures of Europe Microlithic elements are by no means entirely absent.

In arguing thus in favour of independent parallel evolution rather than diffusion as an explanation for the various Microlithic cultures, I do not mean to deny the possibility that diffusion played some part, for I believe that in most problems of this sort where two diametrically opposite views are held, the truth usually lies in a combination of both.

If we turn next to the Neolithic cultures in which polished axes, tanged and other forms of arrow-heads, and a knowledge of agriculture and domestic animals are found, the question of the relative parts played by diffusion and independent evolution is still more difficult to decide, and I do not feel that I am in a position to offer any opinion, but will content myself with quoting a sentence from Breuil, who believes that 'The Neolithic . . . civilizations

of Egypt have also certainly on a number of different
occasions sent out powerful influences over the whole of
North Africa and the great forest regions : but only certain
of these elements reached as far as South Africa.'

In support of this view we may recall that at least one
Neolithic culture of East Africa is associated with beads
of Egyptian origin, while some of the polished axes of
another East African Neolithic culture, the Njoroan, are
very like examples from the Sudan where Egyptian
influence is strong.

If we turn from the Stone Age cultures to the fossil
remains of Stone Age man, we find that here again we
seem to be faced with evidence that in part is favourable
to the diffusionist idea and in part to the idea of parallel
evolution. The great shell-mounds of East and South
Africa seem to represent, for the most part, the living sites
of a race whose culture was a degenerate form of Wilton
and whose physical features recall the Bushmen, except
that in size these shell-mound people were gigantic as
compared with the Bushmen of a few centuries ago.

The shell-mounds of North Africa, on the other hand,
are many of them associated with a Capsian culture,
although there are some that belong to the Mesolithic and
Neolithic derivatives of the Capsian. Physically, the
makers of the North African shell-mound cultures are
quite unlike those who were responsible in East and
South Africa. In Europe in Mesolithic times there were
also races who fed largely on mollusca and left great shell-
mounds behind them, but there seems no reason whatever
for regarding this great chain of shell-mounds from Europe
to South Africa as due to diffusion from a single centre.

In speaking of the cultures, we noticed that the Levalloisian culture is widespread in Africa. In Europe and
Palestine we know that it was made by men of the

Neanderthal species; in Africa, however, we have as yet no positive evidence to show what type of man was the maker of the various local forms of true Levalloisian, so that we cannot say if the spread of the Levalloisian culture was due to migrations or to a spread of influence only, or even if it was possibly a local parallel evolution. The fact that the men associated with some of the 'Middle Stone Age' cultures of South Africa are of *Homo sapiens* type does not preclude the possibility that the race responsible for the purest Levalloisian elements was of a Neanderthal type, for the Middle Stone Age cultures are most of them the results of culture contacts.

As regards the makers of the great Chelleo-Acheulean culture, such human remains as have in Europe been claimed to represent this people are all of a primitive *Homo sapiens* type, but all of them have been put on one side as doubtful specimens, very largely because of the deep-rooted and preconceived ideas that *Homo sapiens* is a recently evolved species, that ought not to be found in Middle Pleistocene deposits. As I have shown in Chapter IX, the theoretical evidence all favours an early age for *Homo sapiens*, and my own personal conviction is that a number of human skull fragments of *Homo sapiens* type in Europe which have been 'put on the shelf' are true examples of the makers of the hand-axe culture.

The East African human remains of Lower and Middle Pleistocene age are at present *sub judice*, but I personally have not the slightest doubts about their authenticity.

As a result of the work that has been carried out in different parts of Africa in the last decade, we now know nearly as much about the culture sequences of the Stone Age in that great continent as we do for the continent of Europe. In Europe as well as in Africa there are big areas concerning which we know very little, and we certainly know more about the Neolithic cultures in Europe than we do in Africa, but gradually the story is becoming clearer, and in a remarkable way the evidence from these two continents is fitting together and helping us to get a better picture of the Stone Age of Europe and Africa as a whole.

Such information as we have from Asia—apart from Palestine we have still very little information about Stone Age cultures found in datable deposits—suggests that the story of the Stone Age in Asia will prove complementary to that of Europe and Africa.

BIBLIOGRAPHY

CHAPTER I

1. 'Changes in the Physical Geography of East Africa in Human Times', by L. S. B. Leakey in *The Geographical Journal*, vol. lxxxiv, 1934.
2. 'Rifts, Rivers, Rains, and Early Man in Uganda', by E. J. Wayland in *Journal of Royal Anthropological Institute*, vol. lxiv, 1934.
3. 'Climatic Pulsations', by Ellsworth Huntingdon in *Geografiska Annaler*, 1935.
4. *World Climate during the Quaternary Period*, by G. C. Simpson, 1934.
5. 'Traces of Ancient Changes of Climate in East Africa', by Erik Nilsson in *Geografiska Annaler, Häfte* 1-2, 1935.
6. 'Royal Anthropological Institute Prehistoric Research Expedition to Kharga Oasis; Preliminary outline of season's work', by G. Caton-Thompson in *Man*, 1931, No. 91.
7. 'The Prehistoric Geography of Kharga Oasis', by G. Caton-Thompson and E. W. Gardener in *The Geographical Journal*, vol. lxxx, no. 5, 1932.
8. 'Les Plissements Acheuléo-Moustériens des Aluvions de Gafsa', by R. Vaufray in *Revue de Géographie physique*, vol. v, fasc. 3, 1932.
9. 'L'Homme fossile d'Asselar', in Mémoire No. 9 of the *Archives de Paléontologie humaine*, Paris, 1932. (Notes on climate of Sahara.)
10. 'La Question des Isthmes Méditerranéens Pléistocènes', by R. Vaufray in *Revue de Géographie Physique*, December, 1929.
11. 'The Quaternary Changes of Ocean Level', by Cosmo Johns in *Geological Magazine*, vol. lxxi, 1934.
12. 'An Examination of the Tertiary and Quaternary Changes in Sea-Level in South Africa', by A. V. Krige in *Annals of the University of Stellenbosch*, 1927.
13. 'The Problem of Past Climates', by A. V. Krige in *South African Journal of Science*, vol. xxix, 1932.
14. 'Changes of Climate in Southern Rhodesia during later Geological Times', by H. B. Maufe in *South African Geological Journal*, vol. xiii, 1930.

15. 'The Physical History of the Victoria Falls', by A. Molyneux in *Geographical Journal*, 1905.
16. 'Climate and Man in Africa', by J. C. Smuts in *South African Journal of Science*, 1932.
17. 'African Pluvial Periods and Prehistoric Man', by E. J. Wayland in *Man*, vol. xxix, 1929.
18. *The Development and Distribution of the African Fauna in connection with and depending on Climatic Changes*, by E. Lönnberg, Stockholm, 1929.
19. *Climate through the Ages*, by C. E. P. Brooks.
20. *Preliminary Report on the Quaternary Geology of Mount Elgon and some parts of the Rift Valley*, by Erik Nilsson.
21. 'Past Climates', by C. S. Simpson in paper to the British Science Guild, 1929.
22. *Quaternary Glaciations and Pluvial Lakes in British East Africa*, by Erik Nilsson, Stockholm, 1932.
23. 'East African Lakes', by L. S. B. Leakey in *Geographical Journal*, vol. lxxvii, June, 1931.
24. Annual Reports of the Geological Survey Department, Uganda, 1927 and 1929.
25. *Palaeolithic Man and the Nile Faiyum Divide* (1929); *Palaeolithic Man and the Nile Valley in Nubia and Upper Egypt* (1923); *Palaeolithic Man and the Nile Valley in Upper and Middle Egypt* (1934). All by K. S. Sandford and W. J. Arkell in Oriental Institute Publications of the University of Chicago.
26. *The Desert Fayum*, by G. Caton-Thompson and E. W. Gardener, a special publication of the Royal Anthropological Institute in 1934.
27. 'The M-horizon, a Result of a Climatic Oscillation in the Second Pluvial Period', by E. J. Wayland in *Bulletin No. 2 of the Geological Survey of Uganda*, 1935.
28. *Glacials and Pluvials*, by S. A. Huzayyin in *Man*, Jan. 1936.

CHAPTER II

1. 'Further Notes on the Archaeology of Sheppard Island', by C. van Riet Lowe in *South African Journal of Science*, vol. xxvi, p. 665, &c. (List of fauna.)
2. 'The Miocene Beds of Victoria Nyanza', &c., by F. Oswald in *Quarterly Journal of Geological Society*, vol. lxx, June, 1914.

3. 'Description of a Fossil Buffalo from East Africa', by Einar Lönnberg in *Arkiv för Zoologi*, vol. 25 A, no. 17, 1933.

4. 'Note préliminaire sur une nouvelle grotte à ossements des environs d'Alger', by C. Arambourg in *Bulletin de la Société d'Histoire Naturelle de l'Afrique du Nord*, vol. xxiii, 1932.

5. 'Fossil Elephants and Man', by A. T. Hopwood in *Proceedings of the Geologists' Association*, vol. xlvi, 1935.

6. 'The Olduvai Expedition, 1931', by A. T. Hopwood in *Natural History Magazine*, vol. iii, no. 23, 1932.

7. *New Fossil Mammals and Man from South Africa*, by T. F. Dreyer and Alice Lyle, 1931.

8. 'A Fossil Wart-hog from Palestine', by D. M. Bate in *Annals and Magazine of Natural History*, ser. 10, vol. xiii, 1934.

9. 'Neue Genera aus der Oldoway-Fauna', by H. Reck in *Zentralblatt für Mineralogie und Paläontologie*, January, 1935.

10. 'A Tooth of Elephas (cf. Antiquus) from the Vaal River', by S. H. Haughton in *Transactions of Royal Society of South Africa*, vol. xii, 1921.

11. 'A Note on Some Fossils from the Vaal River', by S. H. Houghton in *Transactions of Geological Society of South Africa*, vol. xxiv, 1921.

12. 'On Some South African Fossil Proboscidia', by S. H. Houghton in *Transactions of Royal Society of South Africa*, vol. xxii, 1934.

13. 'The Mastodon in the Pleistocene of South Africa', by R. Beck in *Geological Magazine*, 1906.

14. 'Mammoths and Other Fossil Elephants of the Vaal and Limpopo Watersheds', by R. Dart in *South African Journal of Science*, vol. xxvi, 1929.

15. 'On Evidence of a Large Horse recently Extinct', by R. Broom in *South African Annals of South African Museum*, vol. vii, 1909.

16. 'Man Contemporaneous with Extinct Animals', by R. Broom in *Annals of South African Museum*, vol. xii, 1913.

17. 'Notes on Equus capensis', by R. Broom in *Bulletin of American Museum of Natural History*, vol. xxxii, 1913.

18. 'Mammoths and Man in the Transvaal', H. F. Osborn in *Nature*, vol. cxx, p. 41, 1927.

19. 'An African Occurrence of Fossil Mammalia associated with Stone Implements', by F. P. Mennel in *Geological Magazine*, October, 1907.
20. 'Pleistocene Mammals of Algeria', by A. S. Romer in *Belloit College Bulletin*, vol. xxiv, no. 5.
    NOTE. This paper by A. S. Romer contains a very full bibliography of the fauna of North Africa, and should be referred to.
21. 'A Review of the Fossil Mammals of Central Africa', by A. T. Hopwood in *American Journal of Science*, vol. xvii, 1929.
22. 'Primitive Archidiskodon and Palaeoloxodon of South Africa', by H. F. Osborn in *American Museum Novitates*, no. 741, 1934.

CHAPTERS III AND IV

1. *The Stone Age Cultures of Kenya Colony*, by L. S. B. Leakey, 1931.
2. 'Rifts, Rivers, Rains, and Early Man in Uganda', by E. J. Wayland in *Journal of Royal Anthropological Institute*, vol. lxiv, 1934.
3. 'The Magosian Culture of Uganda', by E. J. Wayland and M. C. Burkitt in *Journal of Royal Anthropological Institute*, vol. lxii, 1932.
4. 'The Stone Age in Uganda', by E. J. Wayland in *Man*, vol. xxiv, 1924.
5. 'Some Obsidian Implements from Kenya Colony', by H. Dewey and C. W. Hobley in *Man*, vol. xxv, 1925.
6. 'An Outline of the Stone Age in Kenya', by L. S. B. Leakey in *South African Journal of Science*, vol. xxvi, 1929.
7. 'The Sequence of Stone Age Cultures in East Africa', by L. S. B. Leakey in *Essays presented to C. G. Seligman*, 1934.
8. *Quaternary Glaciations and Pluvial Lakes in British East Africa*, by Erik Nilsson, Stockholm, 1932.
9. *The Stone Age Races of Kenya*, by L. S. B. Leakey, 1935 (Chapter I).

CHAPTER V

1. 'Further Notes on the Archaeology of Sheppard Island', by C. van Riet Lowe in *South African Journal of Science*, vol. xxvi, 1929.

2. 'The Cape Flats Complex', by A. S. H. Goodwin in *South African Journal of Science*, vol. xxx, 1933.

3. 'A New Variation of Smithfield Culture', by E. C. Chubb, G. Burnham King, and A. O. D. Mogg in *Transactions of Royal Society of South Africa*, vol. xxii, part iv.

4. 'Giant Crescents', by C. van Riet Lowe in *Transactions of Royal Society of South Africa*, vol. xix, part ii, 1931.

5. 'Early Man in South Africa', by T. F. Dreyer in *Nature*, April, 1935.

6. 'Premières impressions de voyage sur la préhistoire Sud-Africaine', by Abbé Breuil in *L'Anthropologie*, vol. xl, 1930.

7. 'Notes on Some Polished and Ground Stone Implements from the North-West Karoo', *South African Journal of Science*, vol. xxiii, 1926.

8. 'A Palaeolithic Settlement at Kynsna', by C. van Riet Lowe in *Science Society Journal*, 1922.

9. 'Notes on Some Stone Implements from Tuinsplatts, Springbok Flats', by C. van Riet Lowe in *South African Journal of Science*, vol. xxvi, 1929.

10. 'Fresh Light on the Prehistoric Archaeology of South Africa', by C. van Riet Lowe in *Bantu Studies*, 1930.

11. 'Implimentiferous Gravels of the Vaal River at Riverview Estates', by C. van Riet Lowe in *Nature*, vol. 136, p. 53.

12. 'Chronology of the Mossel Bay Industry', by A. S. H. Goodwin in *South African Journal of Science*, 1930.

13. 'Neolithic Stone Implements found at Regina, Western Transvaal', by M. Orford in *Transactions of Royal Society of South Africa*, vol. xxii, 1934.

14. 'Some Account of a Pebble Industry in the Transvaal', by E. J. Wayland in *Transactions of Royal Society of South Africa*, vol. xvii, 1929.

15. 'A Commentary on the History and Present Position of South African Prehistory with a full Bibliography', edited by A. J. H. Goodwin and published in *Bantu Studies*, December, 1935.
NOTE. This publication gives a very full bibliography

of South African and Rhodesian Prehistory and should be consulted by those who want a fuller bibliography than I have given.

16. 'L'Afrique préhistorique', by H. Breuil in *Cahiers d'Art*, Paris, 1931.
   NOTE. In the second edition of this study a very full bibliography was added, which should be consulted.

17. 'The Stone Age Cultures of South Africa', by A. J. H. Goodwin and C. van Riet Lowe in *Annals of South African Museum*, vol. xxvii, 1928.

CHAPTER VI

1. 'Collections Africaines du département de préhistoire exotique du Musée d'ethnographie du Trocadéro', by H. Kelley in *Journal de la Société des Africanistes*, vol. iv, 1934.

2. 'Notes sur le Capsien', by R. Vaufray in *L'Anthropologie*, vol. xliii, nos. 5 and 6, 1933.

3. 'Deux Gisements extrêmes d'Ibéromaurusien', by E. G. Gobert. and R. Vaufray in *L'Anthropologie*, vol. xlii, 1932.

4. 'Royal Anthropological Institute Prehistoric Research Expedition to Kharga Oasis; Preliminary outline of season's work', by G. Caton-Thompson in *Man*, 1931, no. 91.

5. 'Royal Anthropological Institute Prehistoric Research Expedition to Kharga Oasis; the Second Season's Discoveries, by G. Caton-Thompson in *Man*, No. 158, 1932.

6. 'Les Plissements Acheuléo-Moustériens des Aluvions de Gafsa', by R. Vaufray in *Revue de Géographie physique*, vol. v, fasc. 3, 1932.

7. 'Kharga Oasis', by G. Caton-Thompson in *Antiquity*, June, 1931.

8. 'L'Afrique Préhistorique', by Abbé H. Breuil in *Cahiers d'Art*, 1931.

9. *Palaeolithic Man and the Nile Faiyum Divide* (1929); *Palaeolithic Man and the Nile Valley in Nubia and Upper Egypt* (1923); *Palaeolithic Man and the Nile Valley in Upper and Middle Egypt* (1934). All by K. S. Sandford and W. J. Arkell in Oriental Institute Publications of the University of Chicago.

10. *The Desert Fayum*, by G. Caton-Thompson and E. W. Gardener, a special publication of the Royal Anthropological Institute, in 1934.

11. *Une nouvelle industrie lithique, le Sébilien*, by A. Vignard, Cairo, 1923.

12. 'L'Afrique préhistorique', by H. Breuil in *Cahiers d'Art*, Paris, 1931.
    NOTE. In the second edition of this study a very full bibliography was added, which should be consulted.

13. Mémoire No. 13 of *Archives de l'Institut de Paléontologie humaine*, Paris, 1934.

CHAPTER VII

1. 'Gwelo Kopje', by T. Gardner and P. Stapleton in *Proceedings of Rhodesia Scientific Association*, vol. xxxiii, 1934.

2. 'The Rhodesian Origin of Certain Smithfield Elements', by A. J. H. Goodwin in *Proceedings of Rhodesia Scientific Association*, vol. xxiv, 1934.

3. 'Excavations at Nswatugiand Madiliyangwa', by Neville Jones in *Occasional Paper of the Rhodesian Museum*, April, 1933.

4. 'Notes on Three Groups of Stone Implements from Southern Rhodesia', by A. J. H. Goodwin in *Proceedings of Rhodesia Scientific Association*, vol. xxix, 1929.

5. 'Stone Implements of Palaeolithic and Neolithic Types from Nigeria', by H. J. Braunholtz, Occasional Paper No. 4 of *Geological Survey of Nigeria*, 1926.

6. *The Stone Age in Rhodesia*, by Neville Jones, 1926.

7. 'On the Palaeolithic Deposits of Sawmills, Rhodesia', by Neville Jones in *Journal of Royal Anthropological Institute*, vol. liv, 1924.

8. 'The Middle Stone Age of Rhodesia', by Neville Jones in *Occasional Paper of the Rhodesian Museum*, no. 1, 1932.

9. 'Further Excavations at Gokomere, Southern Rhodesia', by Neville Jones in *Man*, vol. xxxvi, 197.

10. 'Notes on the Occurrence of Stone Implements in the Valley of the Zambesi round Victoria Falls', by G. W. Lamplugh in *Journal of Royal Anthropological Institute*, vol. xxxvi, 1906.

11. 'Rhodesian Cave Expedition', by A. C. Armstrong in *Proceedings of the Prehistoric Society of East Anglia*, 1929.

12. 'Rhodesian Archaeological Expedition, 1929, Excavations in Bambata Cave', &c., by A. C. Armstrong in *Journal of Royal Anthropological Institute*, vol. lxi, 1931.

13. 'Notes on an Implement of Palaeolithic Type from the Victoria Falls, Zambesi', by H. Balfour in *Journal of Royal Anthropological Institute*, vol. xxxvi, 1906.

14. 'L'Afrique Préhistorique', by Abbé H. Breuil in *Cahiers d'Art*, 1931.

15. 'Excavations in a Wilton Industry at Gokomere, Southern Rhodesia', by T. Gardner in *Journal of Royal Anthropological Institute*, vol. lviii, 1928.

16. 'The Stone Age in Northern Rhodesia', by F. B. McCrae in *Nada*, 1926.

17. 'Die Tumbakultur am unteren Kongo', &c., by O. Menghin in *Anthropos*, vol. xx, 1925.

18. 'Instruments de pierre du Congo, Collection Haas', by V. Jacques in *Bulletin de la Société d'Anthropologie*, Bruxelles, 1900.

19. 'L'Afrique préhistorique', by H. Breuil in *Cahiers d'Art*, Paris, 1931.

NOTE. In the second edition of this study a very full bibliography was added, which should be consulted.

CHAPTER VIII

1. 'Œuf d'Autruche gravé et peint du Territoire des Ouled Djebbal', by Abbé Breuil and Dr. Clergeau in *L'Anthropologie*, vol. xli, 1931.

2. 'Premières Impressions de Voyage sur la Préhistoire Sud-Africaine', by H. Breuil in *L'Anthropologie*, vol. xl, 1930.

3. *South Africa's Past in Stone and Paint*, by M. C. Burkitt, 1926.

4. 'Les Gravures Rupestres du Djebel Ouenat', by Prince Kemal el Dine and M. H. Breuil in *Revue des Sciences*, 1928.

5. 'Paintings and Artefacts in Rock Shelters in the Cala District', in *Records of the Albany Museum*, vol. iv, 1931.

6. 'Illustrated Analysis of Prehistoric Rock Paintings from Peltyers Rust', by C. van Reit Lowe in *Transactions of Royal Society of South Africa*, vol. xx, 1931.

7. 'The Age of Rock Engravings in South Africa', by C. van Reit Lowe in *South African Journal of Science*, vol. xxx, 1933.
8. 'Traces of Former Bushmen Occupation in Tanganyika', by D. Bleek in *South African Journal of Science*, 1931.
9. 'L'Afrique Préhistorique', by Abbé H. Breuil in *Cahiers d'Art*, 1931.
10. *Bushman Art*, by H. Obermaier and H. Kuhn, 1930.
11. 'Rock Paintings of the Kangeju Bushmen of Tanganyika Territory', by F. Bagshawe in *Man*, vol. xxiii, 1923.
12. 'L'Art Africain', by Leo Frobenius in *Cahiers d'Art*, 1930 and 1931.
13. 'Note on the Discovery of Some Rock Paintings near Kondoa Irangi', by T. A. M. Nash in *Journal of Royal Anthropological Institute*, vol. lix, 1929.
14. *Bushmen Paintings*, by H. Tongue, 1909.
15. 'L'Afrique préhistorique', by H. Breuil in *Cahiers d'Art*, Paris, 1931.
    NOTE. In the second edition of this study a very full bibliography was added, which should be consulted.
16. A commentary on the history and present position of South African Prehistory with a full bibliography, edited by A. J. H. Goodwin and published in *Bantu Studies*, December, 1935.
    NOTE. This publication gives a very full bibliography of South African and Rhodesian Prehistory and should be consulted by those who want a fuller bibliography than I have given.
17. 'The Palaeolithic Art of North-East Spain and the Art of Bushmen: 'A Comparison', by H. Breuil in *Man*, Sept.1930.
18. 'L'Âge de l'art rupestre nord-africain, by H. Obermaier in *L'Anthropologie*, 1931, vol. xli.
19. 'Peintures rupestres préhistoriques du Harrar (Abyssinie)', by H. Breuil in *L'Anthropologie*, vol. xliv, 1934.

CHAPTER IX

1. 'L'Homme fossile d'Asselar', in Mémoire No. 9 of *Archives de Paléontologie humaine*, Paris, 1932.
2. 'An Australoid Skull from the Cape Flats', by M. R. Drennan in *Journal of Royal Anthropological Institute*, vol. lix, 1929.

206   BIBLIOGRAPHY

3. 'Early Man in South Africa', by T. F. Dreyer in *Nature*, 20 April 1935.

4. 'Floris Bad Man', by T. F. Dreyer and Ariens Kappers in *Kon. Akad.*, Amsterdam, 1935.

5. 'Un Ossuaire Humain de Paléolithique supérieur en Afrique du Nord', by C. Arambourg in *Comptes Rendus* of the 55th Session of the Association Française pour l'Avancement des Sciences, 1931.

6. 'Skeletal Material from Early Graves in the Riet Valley', by L. H. Wells and J. H. Gear in *South African Journal of Science*, vol. xxviii, 1931.

7. 'The Cliff Dwellers of Zitzikama', by F. W. Fitzsimons in *Illustrated London News*, December, 1921.

8. 'The Cliff Dwellers of Tzitzekama, Result of Recent Excavations', in *South African Journal of Science*, vol. xxiii.

9. 'The Evidence for the Age of *Homo Rhodesiensis*', by F. P. Mennel in *South African Journal of Science*, vol. xxvi, 1929.

10. *Rhodesian Man and Associated Remains*, by W. P. Pyecraft and others, British Museum publication, 1928.

11. Mémoire No. 13 of *Archives de l'Institut de Paléontologie humaine*, Paris, 1934.

12. *The Stone Age Races of Kenya*, by L. S. B. Leakey, 1935.

13. *New Discoveries relating to the Antiquity of Man*, by Sir Arthur Keith, 1931.

14. 'Untersuchungen über den Oldowayfund', by Geisler and Mollison in *Verhandlungen der Gesellschaft für Physische Anthropologie*, Band III.

15. 'Prähistorische Grab- und Menschenfunde und ihre Beziehungen zur Pluvialzeit in Ostafrika', by H. Reck in *Mitteilungen aus den deutschen Schutzgebieten*, Band XXXIV, Berlin, 1926.

16. Letters to *Nature* by various authors, vol. 128, 24 October 1931; vol. 128, 26 December 1931; vol. 129, 27 February 1932; vol. 129, 14 May 1932; vol. 130, 18 March 1933.

17. 'Early Human Remains in East Africa', Report of a Conference held at Cambridge in *Man*, no. 16, 1933.

18. Letter by P. G. H. Boswell in *Nature*, 9 March 1933.

19. 'L'Âge des Hommes fossiles de Metch El-Arbi', by R. Vaufrey in *Bulletin de la Société Historique et géographique de la Région de Sétif*, 1936.

INDEX

SOUTH AFRICA, Stone Age cultures of, Chapter V.
SOUTHERN RHODESIA, 94, 169.
— — cultures of, 121 et seq.
— — prehistoric art of, 189.
— — Stone Age art of, 137 et seq.
SPAIN, 185.
— EASTERN, art of, 189.
— Aurignacian culture in, 186.
— cultures of, compared with N. Africa, 106.
SPRINGBOK FLATS, skull from, 167, 173.
STAPLETON, Father, 121.
STEOTOPYGA, emphasis of, in paintings, 143.
STELLENBOSCH CULTURE, 122, 166, 181.
— — discussion of, 80 et seq.
— — in S. Africa, 78.
— — UPPER, fauna of (footnote), 34.
STILLBAY, site at, 94.
— CULTURE, 96, 119, 122, 140, 187, 191, 192.
— — at Apis Rock, 63 et seq.
— — comparison with Aterian, 105.
— — from Fishoek, 169.
— — from Somaliland, 128.
STONE AGE, climate of, in Africa, 4 et seq.
— — climate of, in Europe and Africa, 16.
— — ART, differences between Africa and Europe, 145.
— — — discussion of origin, 161.
— — — of Africa and Europe compared, 189 et seq.
— — CULTURES of S. Africa, Chapter V.
— — — in S. Africa, table of, 97.
— — — of French N. Africa, summarized, 112 et seq.
— — — of S. Africa, 78.
— — — of S. Rhodesia (table), 123.
— — — of India, 130.
STONE BOWLS of Gumban culture, 70.

STRAND-LOOPERS, burials, 150.
— 159.
— skulls of, 167.
STRIPED HYAENA, in N. Africa, 24.
STYLES OF ENGRAVINGS, sequence of, in S. Africa, 143 et seq.
— — PAINTING, sequence of, at Bambata, 138 et seq.
— — sequence of, in S. Africa, 141 et seq.
— — sequence of, in E. Africa, 152 et seq.
SUDAN, the, 70, 194.
— prehistory of, 131.
Sus scrofa, the wild boar still living in N. Africa, 19.
SUSSEX, 163.

TABELBALAT, ancient lake basin of, 102.
TACHENGHIT culture, 102.
TAFERJIT, site at, 112.
TAMAYA MELLET, Neolithic culture of, 120.
— — site at, 112.
TANGANYIKA LAKE, terraces of, 127.
— TERRITORY, 9, 38, 59, 62, 74. seq.
— — cave-paintings in, 150 et seq.
— — Highlands of, 2.
— — Pleistocene fauna of, 27 et seq.
— — prehistoric art of, 190.
'TANGED MOUSTERIAN', 105.
TARDENOISIAN CULTURE, 107, 192.
TASIAN CULTURE of Egypt, 120.
TAUNGS SKULL, age of, 35.
TEILHARD, Father, 128.
TEL-EL-AMARNA, beads from, 70.
TERNIFINE, site at, 101.
THOMPSON, Miss Caton, 27, 114.
TIMBUCTOO, 177.
TONGUE, Miss H., 141.
'TORTOISE CORE', 62.
TRANSVAAL, Boskop site in, 167.
— pebble culture in, 81.
— the, 79.
TRINIL, JAVA, 163.
TROIS FRÈRES, masked figure from, 144.

218 INDEX

TSANA, LAKE, 4.
TUMBA, site at, 71, 132.
TUMBIAN, of the Congo, 111.
TUMBIAN CULTURE, 56, 71, 98, 132, 175.
— — discussion of, 72.
— — in Kenya, 134.
TUNIS, 184, 192.
TZITZIKAMA, skulls from, 167.

UGANDA, 66, 71.
— chimpanzees in, 21.
— geological survey of, 38.
— gorillas in, 21.
— Stone Age studies in, 9.
— PROTECTORATE, 132.
— — Pleistocene fauna of, 27 et seq.
UMVUKWES, paintings of, 143.
'UPLIFT' MOVEMENTS, evidence of, 10.
UPPER AURIGNACIAN, associated human remains, 172.
UPPER PLEISTOCENE in E. Africa, cultures of, Chapter IV.

VAAL VALLEY, 83.
— RIVER, terrace gravels of, 79.
— — terraces of, 12.
VALLOIS, Prof., 175, 177 et seq.
VAN HOEPEN, E. C. (footnote), 35.
VAN RIET LOWE, Prof., 32 et seq., 77, 88 et seq.
VAUFREY, Prof. R., 5, 9, 101, 104 (footnote), 106 et seq., 110, 175, 184, 190.
VEREENIGING, site at, 84.
VICTORIA FALLS, 4, 14.
— — famous site at, 121, 124 et seq.
— NYANZA, 48, 68.
— — Lake, 3, 134, 150.
VICTORIA WEST, cores of, 88.
— — technique, 82 et seq.
VIGNARD, M., 114, 119.
VOLCANOES, 3.
— in Africa, 8.

WANA, in Nigeria, Microlithic culture from, 136.
WART HOGS, 21.
— — in N. Africa, 24.
WATER BUCK, in N. Africa, 25.
WATER BUFFALO, in Late Pleistocene, 35.
— — of Asiatic type in E. Africa, 32.
— — of Asiatic type in Africa, 37.
WAYLAND, Mr. E. J., 9, 10, 38 et seq., 52, 57 (footnote), 66, 80.
WELLCOME MUSEUM, 131.
WEST AFRICA, 12.
— — the fauna of, 20 et seq.
— — fauna of to-day, 19.
WILD BOAR, living in N. Africa, 19.
WILDEBEEST, 21.
WILMAN, Miss M., 144.
WILTON, 137.
— A, 68.
— B, 68.
— culture, 96 et seq., 169.
— — associated human remains, 174.
— — discussion of its divisions, 69.
— — distribution of, 192.
— — from Somaliland, 128.
— — from Tanganyika, 158.
— — of Rhodesia, 123, 193.
— — painting associated with, 191.
— of Kenya, Stage B, 65.
WINDSORTON, site at, 82 et seq., 88.
WOLVES, Pleistocene species surviving, 19.
WORTHINGTON, Dr. E. B., zoological work at Lake Rudolph, 14.

ZAMBESI, RIVER, 4, 14, 126.
— terraces of, 12.
ZEBRA, 21.
— in E. Africa, 28.
— in engraving in Rhodesia, 143.
ZWIGLAR, Mr., 170.